The
Instant Pot®
College
Cookbook

The Instant Pot® College Cookbook

75 Quick & Easy Meals That Taste Like Home

JULEE MORRISON

PHOTOGRAPHY BY EVI ABELER

ROCKRIDGE PRESS

For general information on our other products and services or to obtain technical support, please contact our Customer Care Department within the United States at (866) 744-2665, or outside the United States at (510) 253-0500.

Rockridge Press publishes its books in a variety of electronic and print formats. Some content that appears in print may not be available in electronic books, and vice versa.

TRADEMARKS: Rockridge Press and the Rockridge Press logo are trademarks or registered trademarks of Callisto Media Inc. and/or its affiliates, in the United States and other countries, and may not be used without written permission. All other trademarks are the property of their respective owners. Rockridge Press is not associated with any product or vendor mentioned in this book.

Interior and Cover Designer: Suzanne LaGasa
Editor: Stacy Wagner-Kinnear
Production Editor: Erum Khan
Cover and Interior Photography by Evi Abeler, © 2018, food styling by Albane Sharrard; except © Nicepix/Shutterstock, p. 13

ISBN: Print 978-1-64152-259-5   eBook 978-1- 64152-260-1

This book is dedicated to the kitchen table,
where my mother put love on our plates,
Charlotte the Great told stories that kept us
in our seats, my children's laughter echoes,
friends gather, and my husband keeps coming
back no matter what I serve.

xoxo

CONTENTS

INTRODUCTION

Like many people, I learned to cook from the earlier generations of women in my family.

My great-grandmother passed down her bread- and pie-baking expertise. My grandmother taught me to can pickles and make lasagna from scratch. And my mother, who taught herself butchery in her own restaurant kitchen, passed on an understanding of the science of cooking.

Now it's my turn to teach my six children about food, recipes, and cooking techniques. On my first trip to visit my oldest son, Jake, in college, he made me a chicken bowl that wowed me with layers of flavors and texture, so I guess they've learned something from me over the years. But one thing is clear: My kids don't have the time, patience, or inclination for the kind of cooking my family taught me. The world moves too fast these days for them to commit to long, drawn-out cooking processes. Now they want good food, and healthy food, but they want to be able to make it quickly in between all the other things that pull their attention—school, work, extracurriculars, the pressure of finals, and more.

And it's not just time that limits young cooks. When I first moved out of my family home and had to learn to cook for myself, I discovered just how difficult it was to cook traditional recipes in a small space with very little in the way of specialized equipment—and a tight budget to boot. Then there's the issue of various roommates, all trying to use a shared kitchen at the same time.

When you don't have ample space for meal preparation, lengthy ingredient lists are daunting to both your budget and your shopping prowess, and complicated cooking techniques put up constant stumbling blocks, your options are grim. The dining hall and vending machine choices are unsatisfying, and frozen food heated in a microwave isn't much better.

Enter the Instant Pot®, a multifunction electric pressure cooker that's a godsend for our busy lifestyles, making it possible to eat food that is nourishing, healthy, and satisfying even when a hectic schedule leaves little time for cooking. The shared postage stamp—size living space you call home may not seem to offer many dining options, but an Instant Pot® quickly shifts those options from bleak to sleek.

The more I use my Instant Pot®, the more I enjoy cooking. If I get inspiration for a new recipe, the Instant Pot® is receptive and gives almost immediate gratification. I can spin my idea and 20 minutes later, in most instances, it's there, ready to eat. You don't need much space at all to cook with an Instant Pot®. An end table or the corner of the desk is all you need to set one up. Then you're on your way to ready-to-go lunches and homemade dinners with plenty of menu options in between.

Think of the interior of the Instant Pot® as a blank slate for showcasing your favorite foods—American favorites like Sloppy Joes (page 91) and Spaghetti and Meatballs (page 89), and popular international dishes like Arroz con Pollo (page 73) and Teriyaki Chicken (page 82). It really does all the work for you. There are so many possibilities for your menu that you'll never get into a rut: soup, chili, beans, rice, chicken, and anything else you crave.

The Instant Pot® is also healthier because it puts you in control, which means less sugar, sodium, and processed foods. It doesn't matter if you're a carnivore; eating Paleo, vegan, gluten-free; or just trying to eat better. The Instant Pot® is the answer for healthy food fast. On top of that, you'll save money by avoiding the lure of takeout when you're hungry and short on time.

Your space, your time, and your budget may be minimal, but with the Instant Pot®, your menu is limited only by your imagination. This cookbook is filled with delicious recipes that are great for any day of the week. Each recipe contains ingredients that are usually easy to find in any grocery story, or offers substitution tips for any hard-to-find items. This cookbook will guide you through your cooking journey. So, go ahead, choose a recipe and let's get started! Your Instant Pot® is ready.

CHAPTER 1

Good Fast Food

A few years ago, my family relocated. Our new living situation was meant to be temporary, but we were there for four years. The kitchen was barely usable for one person, let alone a large family. It had a two-foot-wide countertop that served as the only prep area, and turning on the oven heated the entire house. Cooking was challenging, to say the least. Then we brought home an Instant Pot®, and our menu expanded to include a wide variety of foods we all loved, rather than being limited to what we could manage with traditional equipment.

The Instant Pot® is a gift to anyone who wants to eat home-cooked food but has limited time, cooking space, and money. While you may have received or purchased an Instant Pot® to help you get meals made fast, it's actually a multicooker with a variety of helpful functions—all models of the Instant Pot® can pressure cook, slow cook, sauté, steam, and cook rice. Certain models even allow you to make your own yogurt. In this book, the majority of recipes will take advantage of the pressure cooker and sauté functions to help you get meals made in short order.

This is the cookbook for you if you're looking to use your Instant Pot® in your dorm (if allowed) or off-campus apartment, while RV camping, or in a temporary or makeshift kitchen. It will show you how to cook satisfying, mostly healthy meals in a fraction of the time they'd take on the stove or in the oven, allowing you to eat well effortlessly so you can live college life to the fullest.

WHY INSTANT POT®?

The Instant Pot® has many great features going for it, but the truth is that it doesn't really cook food in an instant. If fast food is all you're looking for, chances are you have lots of options for getting it. Prepackaged oatmeal can be microwaved in no time, ramen noodles cook up in less than 10 minutes on the stove, and takeout is likely a short drive or delivery away. At some point during your time in college, you'll probably rely on these quick options. But exclusively eating unhealthy fast foods throughout college won't do you any favors, and the cost will add up, especially if takeout becomes something you depend on.

What the Instant Pot® does that really no other kitchen appliance can do is make cooking totally hands off, pretty fast (and certainly faster than any other alternative), and as wholesome as the ingredients you put into it. It doesn't hurt that the Instant Pot®

does a really great job of cooking homemade, more nutritious versions of staples that college students have run on for years, including beans, rice, pasta, and chicken that can be used in everything from tacos to salads to soups. Here are just a few reasons why my own college-age kids love it:

It allows for hands-off cooking: There is no need to babysit the pot to prevent overcooking, and no need to stir constantly to keep the food from burning. Study, text, or watch television while the Instant Pot® cooks.

It saves money: If you have a dining hall meal plan, you never have to think about what you eat—you just show up and fill your plate. But if you're living off campus and have to depend on yourself to get fed, you need to plan ahead. By planning a bit and buying ingredients that you can cook once in the Instant Pot® and get several meals out of, you'll find yourself saving money on food. The Instant Pot® will also save you money on energy bills. It uses much less fuel to heat the Instant Pot® for, say, 30 minutes than to heat your oven for an hour. It also doesn't heat up your apartment, which can mean you'll need less air-conditioning on hot days.

It makes food more flavorful: Cooking under pressure infuses food with flavor. The difference between the same recipes cooked in the Instant Pot® versus on the stove top is remarkable. Rather than boiling food and letting flavors escape through evaporation, the Instant Pot® seals all the flavor in the pot by super-heating the food under pressure. The flavors of your ingredients become deeply infused into the finished dish.

It makes cleanup easy: No one looks forward to washing a ton of kitchen equipment after cooking. While most recipes in this book are likely to require you to dirty a knife, a cutting board, and possibly a measuring cup or spoon during the cooking process, the only big thing that'll head to the sink or dishwasher after cooking is the inner cooking pot of the Instant Pot®. And made of stainless steel, it cleans up very easily.

PRESSURE COOKING 101

So, what exactly is pressure cooking? In short, it's a process in which the buildup of pressure (from steam) is used to cook food. Cooking under pressure is the fastest and most efficient way to cook.

▲ Cooking at **high pressure** is ideal for hearty meals that will power you through long nights of studying or days when you're running around campus from one thing to the next. Think foods like poultry, beef, grains, hard vegetables, and pasta.

▲ Cooking at **low pressure** is recommended for more delicate foods like eggs, for a portable protein-rich snack, and fish, for healthy salads or light dinners. (While fish cook well and quickly at low pressure, they're pretty much just as quick and easy to cook on the stove top, so you won't find recipes for fish in this cookbook.)

Most models of the Instant Pot® allow you to cook at high and low pressure. If you have a LUX model, you can cook at high pressure, but low pressure is not an option.

While stove-top pressure cookers have a reputation for being dangerous or prone to explosions, modern electric pressure cookers like the Instant Pot® feature fail-safe, state-of-the-art safety mechanisms. The Instant Pot® is very safe to use. In fact, it is one of the safest pressure cookers on the market. It features a float valve (see page 8)

Essential Tools

The Instant Pot® doesn't require much additional equipment, but there are some kitchen tools that will make meal prep and cooking easier. In every recipe in this book, you'll see a short equipment section listing the items you'll need (other than the Instant Pot®) to pull off the recipe. Here are some of the types of equipment you'll see:

* Aluminum foil
* Plastic wrap
* Can opener
* Steamer basket
* Wooden spoon or silicone spatula
* Cutting board
* Knives
* Mixing bowls—small, medium, and large
* Measuring cups and spoons
* Whisk
* Tongs
* Springform pan (a 7-inch springform pan can fit into the 3-, 6-, or 8-quart Instant Pot®)

with a pin-lock mechanism that keeps the lid locked if there is pressure inside. In other words, when the lid is on and in the "sealing" position, a seal is established between the lid and the cooker base, creating an airtight chamber. As heat is applied to the inner cooking pot, pressure increases until it reaches full pressure, at which point the float valve seals the pressure inside the chamber. The lid is locked and can't be removed until the pressure is safely released through the pressure release valve.

FOODS TO PRESSURE COOK

The Instant Pot® shines when cooking eggs, hard vegetables, grains, beans, poultry, and beef. You can cook up literally a dozen hard-boiled eggs in 15 minutes. Add just about 5 minutes to that to go from opening a bag of rice to enjoying a steaming bowlful. You can use the Instant Pot® to cook chicken breasts perfectly (see the recipe for Chicken Caesar Salad on page 70), and then use the meat in an endless array of meals, from tacos and soups, to salads and sandwiches.

Is there anything the Instant Pot® can't—or shouldn't—cook? Yes: The Instant Pot® is not ideal for making crispy foods. Because it cooks foods by steaming, you won't achieve the same texture as with the oven. I also prefer to cook steak on the grill or under the broiler. Delicate foods like fish and shellfish often turn out better and cook faster using traditional methods. For that reason, you won't find any seafood recipes in this book.

PARTS OF THE POT

It's good to learn a bit of Instant Pot® vocabulary before jumping into the recipes. Getting familiar with the appliance itself will introduce you to most of the terms. Here are the parts of the Instant Pot® that you should know:

Inner Cooking Pot: This is the pot you'll actually cook your food in. You'll place it inside the cooker before cooking anything, add ingredients and liquid to it, and remove it after cooking to clean. It features a food-grade stainless steel, triple-ply bottom to distribute heat evenly. It is both FDA-compliant and dishwasher-safe.

Cooker Base: This is the part of the Instant Pot® that that contains the heating element and microprocessor. Never place anything inside the cooker base without first inserting the stainless steel inner cooking pot. The cooker base should never be immersed in water for cleaning. If necessary, wipe the exterior clean.

Lid: The lid has a handle on top that you'll hold to lock the lid into place before cooking and unlock after cooking. On the lid itself is an arrow to show you the direction for locking. Once the lid is locked, it cannot be unlocked during the cooking process, as a safety mechanism. It can be unlocked and removed only once all of the pressure has been released and the float valve (see page 8) drops. The lid is rather large and can take up space when set down after cooking, but you can store it vertically in either of the side handles of the Instant Pot®.

Sealing Ring: Also referred to as a gasket, the silicone sealing ring is seated in the underside of the pressure cooker lid. It provides an airtight seal so your pot can come to pressure. It can, and should, be removed for cleaning. The pot won't come up to pressure without it, so always check to make sure it is in position before beginning to cook.

Pressure Release Valve: This is the wobbly knob with holes on the top of the lid. Steam passes through this valve as the pot builds pressure. Turning this valve to the "sealing" position seals the pressure inside the pot. Turning the valve to the "venting" position releases the pressure. The "venting" position

SEALING RING

COOKER BASE

Instant Pot®
www.InstantPot.com

00:05

Low Pressure   High Pressure

Less   Normal   More

Broth

Meat
Stew

Bean
Chili

Sauté

Rice

Multigrain

Porridge

Steam

Slow
Cook

Pressure
Level

Keep
Warm

Yogurt

Sauté

Delay
Start

Cancel

Pressure
Cook

CONDENSATION
COLLECTOR

MEASURING CUP

TRIVET

RICE PADDLE

SOUP SPOON

PRESSURE
RELEASE VALVE

FLOAT VALVE

LID

INNER COOKING POT

is used for some cooking processes, such as slow cooking, which does not rely on the buildup of pressure.

Float Valve/Pin: Every Instant Pot® has a metal pin in the lid that pops up when the Instant Pot® is at pressure. When the pin is up, the lid of the pot is locked for safety. When the pressure is released, the pin drops and the lid unlocks, making it safe to open the lid. Never try to force the lid open if the pin is up.

Trivet: For some recipes, you will place this metal rack in the bottom of the inner cooking pot to keep food above the liquid.

The trivet is also used to hold a pot or bowl above the liquid.

Condensation Collector: This little plastic cup attaches to the back of the pot to collect liquid that drains from the rim of the pot, as well as condensation coming off the valve and the steam release knob housing. Not all models include a condensation collector.

Shield: The removable, perforated metal cover over the steam release valve on the underside of the lid is used to shield the valve from debris that would prevent it from building and releasing pressure.

COOKING THE INSTANT POT® WAY

Whether or not you've had experience cooking for yourself before heading off to college, it's good to get a basic introduction to cooking with the Instant Pot®, which is about as easy as cooking gets.

Cooking Settings

At a glance, the Instant Pot® might look a bit like the dashboard of an alien spaceship with its multiple settings. Truth be told, the recipes in this book require using just a couple of settings over and over, namely Sauté and Pressure Cook (in older models, the Manual setting is what is now called Pressure Cook).

On occasion, recipes will call for what are known as the presets—buttons that read

Poultry, Rice, Yogurt, and so on. These settings have built-in pressure levels and cook times associated with them, so you don't have to think about high pressure versus low pressure, or how long to cook at pressure. Here are the standard settings on most Instant Pot® models, and the cook times and pressure levels associated with them:

Beans: 30 minutes at high pressure.

Eggs: 5 minutes at high pressure (hard-boiled) or 4 minutes at high pressure (soft-boiled).

Meat: 35 minutes at high pressure.

Porridge: 20 minutes at high pressure.

Rice: The rice button is the *only* fully automatic setting; it adjusts the cooking time based on the amount of rice and liquid you add to the inner cooking pot. You can cook as little as 1 cup of rice.

Soup: 30 minutes at high pressure. This setting keeps soup from boiling too rapidly and allows it to simmer, developing the flavor.

Yogurt: This button activates the boil and incubation functions in the yogurt-making process. Press it and you can make regular yogurt and Greek yogurt. Don't let the word "yogurt" limit your possibilities, though— you can also use this button to make ricotta cheese and sour cream, too! The Yogurt setting is included only on the DUO models of Instant Pot®. If you have a LUX, you're out of luck.

Multigrain: 40 minutes at high pressure.

Poultry: 15 minutes at high pressure.

Manual or Pressure Cook: This button allows you to set a specific pressure cooking time, and it's called for most frequently throughout this book. If you have a DUO model, once you've selected the time, you will then adjust the pressure level to High or Low. (Note that the LUX models do not allow you to adjust the pressure manually; all recipes cook at high pressure.)

Sauté: This setting has a default time of 30 minutes, and you can choose the heat level of Less, Normal, More, or Low, Medium, High. You'll use it for browning meat, caramelizing onions, and making cheese sauce.

I tell my kids that the Sauté setting has superpowers: I also use it to preheat my Instant Pot® (warm the liquid as I prepare the dish). In a recipe where I need to prepare the Instant Pot® by adding water to the pot, I press Sauté to heat the water. Then, when I'm ready to start the pressure cooking cycle, I lock the lid into place and set the cooking program. Because the water is already warm or hot, the pot will come to pressure and begin its countdown quicker.

Steam: 10 minutes at high pressure. With this setting, you are typically using a trivet or steamer basket to elevate food above the liquid. (The Instant Pot® will heat continuously, so you don't want anything resting directly on the bottom of the inner cooking pot while cooking.) Use this setting for steaming vegetables, chicken, or eggs.

Keep Warm/Cancel: When cooking is done, the Instant Pot® will automatically activate this feature to keep the inner cooking pot warm. It's active when the timer ends and the display reads L:XX:XX. You'll use this when a recipe says to allow the pressure to release naturally for a certain number of minutes. To turn it off, select Cancel.

When you select a setting such as Pressure Cook or one of the specific functions like Meat or Poultry, the Instant Pot® sets a default time. You can adjust this using the [+] button to increase the time or the [–] button to decrease the time. The Instant Pot® "remembers" the time you last set for a given cooking program. So, if you make a recipe using Pressure Cook, adjust the pressure to High, and set the cooking time to 20 minutes, the next time you select Pressure Cook, the panel will default to High pressure and a cook time of 20 minutes.

Cooking Order

It's easy to get comfortable with the Instant Pot® after a few uses because there's a basic process you'll follow almost every time. Here it is:

1. **Prep the ingredients.** Take a look at the ingredients list for a given recipe and you'll see that the required prep is included there. For example: "1 cup chopped onion" or "1 garlic clove, minced." I know that no one likes to spend tons of time prepping ingredients for a recipe, so I've tried to limit prep as much as possible. That said, reviewing all the prep and doing it first will allow you to move quickly through the rest of the steps.

2. **Precook the ingredients.** You may need to do what's called precooking before you actually cook food under pressure. If so, the recipe will tell you to add ingredients to the inner cooking pot of the Instant Pot® and use the Sauté setting. When you select it, it'll heat the inner cooking pot quickly and allow you to use it as you would a skillet or stockpot on the stove top—to brown meat, sauté onions and other vegetables in oil or butter, and heat or reduce liquids.

3. **Add liquid.** Liquid is crucial when cooking with the Instant Pot®, since cooking at pressure depends on the buildup of steam. Every recipe in this book is written to account for the proper amount of liquid. Liquid can come directly from food (such as canned tomatoes or chicken thighs) or may need to be added (such as water or broth). Always follow instructions for adding liquid exactly; the success of your recipe will depend on it.

4. **Lock the lid and turn the valve to "sealing."** Pressure cooking won't happen if the lid isn't locked into place. Every recipe will note the point at which you should lock the lid into place. Once that's done, make sure you set the release valve to "sealing." If you don't, the valve will remain in the "venting" position, meaning it's open and any steam produced will be released. If that happens, the pot won't come to pressure and your food won't cook.

5. **Select the setting, adjust the pressure, and input the cooking time.** As mentioned before, most of the recipes in this book call for you to select the Pressure Cook setting. You'll then need to adjust the pressure to High or Low, depending on what the recipe says, and then adjust the time up or down until you get to the exact number of minutes called for in the recipe. If you are using a preset, such as Rice

or Poultry, you won't have to worry about adjusting pressure or inputting the cooking time; they're built in. All you'll need to do is select the setting, double-check to make sure your valve is sealed, and walk away.

6. Release the pressure. When pressure cooking is done, your Instant Pot® will beep. At that point, look to the recipe to see which type of pressure release it calls for. The options include *natural release*, *quick release*, and *natural release* followed by a *quick release*.

   ▲ If instructed to use a *natural release*, you won't need to do anything. The cooking time will end and the pressure will start to release on its own. When the float valve drops, you can unlock the lid.

   ▲ If instructed to use a *quick release*, you'll need to carefully switch the pressure release valve from the "sealing" to "venting" position. The quick release of steam will be quite loud, and hot. Avoid putting your face close to the valve when you switch the position, as the steam will be extremely hot.

   ▲ If instructed to use a *natural release* followed by a *quick release*, you'll need to keep an eye on the timer countdown so that you know when to switch the valve to "venting" after the specific natural release time has completed.

7. Unlock the lid and hang it on the handles. The Instant Pot® lid won't unlock until all of the pressure has been released and the float valve— which was pushed up when the pot achieved pressure—drops down. If it's quiet in your apartment, the sound of the valve dropping will be audible.

INSTANT POT® MODELS

All of the recipes in this book were tested in my Instant Pot® IP-DUO60 6-quart 7-in-1 Multi-Functional Pressure Cooker. You may have been given or handed down a 6-quart model, or perhaps you were gifted a 3-quart Mini. As a college student, you'll likely be making smaller-batch recipes for the most part, with perhaps some bulk cooking of staples like rice, beans, and even hard-boiled eggs. Most of the recipes in this book can be cooked in any size or model of Instant Pot®, though in some cases the terminology used may be slightly different. For example, the Ultra model does not have a valve that you need to manually set to sealing or venting—that happens automatically.

The Basics of Amazing Beans and Rice

Beans and rice will go a long way toward keeping you nourished throughout college living. Fortunately, the Instant Pot® shines when it comes to cooking these staples. While the later chapters in this book include recipes for a variety of bean and rice dishes you'll want to make, here's some helpful-to-know info before you head into cooking.

BEANS

Dishes like my Tex-Mex Chili (page 57), refried beans (see the tip on page 38), and many soups require beans. With the Instant Pot®, presoaking beans is a thing of the past, meaning dried beans can be ready to eat in under an hour. (Of course, if you want to presoak your beans, you can certainly do that. Just cut the cooking time listed in the recipe in half.) And on top of the time savings, beans cooked in the Instant Pot® also have a texture that is extra tender and delicious. If you've ever cracked open a can of beans and found those bland, mushy cooked beans to be a turnoff, dried beans cooked in the Instant Pot® will be your new go-to.

Beans are simple, but keep these tips in mind:

* Use 6 to 8 cups of water per pound of dried beans. A pound of dried beans is about 2 cups. Dried beans triple in volume when cooked, so 1 pound (or 2 cups) of dried beans yields about 6 cups of cooked beans.

* In recipes that call for one (15-ounce) can of beans—like Spanish Chili (page 56) or Tex-Mex Chili (page 57)—the equivalent is about 1¾ cups of cooked beans, but you can round up and use 2 cups of cooked beans. Cooking 1 pound of dried beans yields the equivalent of about three cans of beans.

* Because beans will expand when they cook, never fill the pot more than halfway to start.

* Cook beans at high pressure for about 30 minutes, depending on the type of beans. The charts in the back of the book will provide specific times.

* Use a natural pressure release to help the beans retain their shape and skin. If time is an issue, a 10-minute natural pressure release followed by a quick release will be fine.

Test your beans when you unlock and remove the lid of the Instant Pot®. If they are not quite done to your liking, put the lid back on, turn the valve to the "sealing" position, and set the time for 5 minutes if they need just a little more time or 10 minutes if they need even more time. The pot will come to pressure quickly because it's still hot. When the timer beeps, quick release the pressure.

Cooked beans can be stored in an airtight container in the refrigerator for up to 5 days. You can also divide the beans into 1- or 2-cup portions (zip-top freezer bags work great) and store them in the freezer for up to 3 months. Then you'll just thaw them overnight in the refrigerator and they'll be ready to use in any recipe that calls for cooked or canned beans.

You can vary the flavor of your beans by using beef broth, chicken broth, or vegetable broth in place of the water. Or you can add chopped onions or garlic, a bay leaf, and salt or other seasonings to the cooking water. If you're making pinto beans to use for Taco Pie (page 94) or other Mexican-themed dishes, add taco seasoning and salt to the pot along with the beans and water.

RICE

It's easy to cook perfect rice in the Instant Pot®. The result is fluffy, flavorful rice with minimal effort. Most Instant Pot® models have a Rice setting. This is the button for making perfect long-grain white rice in the Instant Pot®. The cooking time will need to be adjusted for other types of rice.

With the following tips, you'll be on your way to perfect pressure cooker rice:

- Use a 1:1 ratio of rice to water (that is the exact same amount of rice as water), regardless of the type of rice you use. This differs from the traditional rice preparation, which calls for a 1:2 ratio of rice to water. With the 1:1 method, you can make as much or as little rice as you want without effort.

- For light, fluffy white rice, rinse the rice before cooking to remove additional starch. Simply place your rice in a fine-mesh strainer and run it under cold water until the water runs clear. Brown rice and other whole-grain rice don't need to be rinsed before cooking.

- Add a little bit of oil to the cooking water because it helps cut down on the "spitting" the Instant Pot® does, and it also keeps the rice from sticking to the bottom of the pot.

- If you are making rice other than long-grain white rice, you'll want to increase your time, but again, the rice-to-water ratio is the same, 1:1. Keep these cooking times in mind for different types of rice:

  - Basmati (white): 4 to 8 minutes
  - Brown (long/short): 21 to 28 minutes
  - Wild rice mix: 25 to 30 minutes

INSTANT POT® PANTRY

The Instant Pot® will cook whatever you put into it, but the flavor depends on the herbs, spices, broths, sauces, and seasonings you use. The better your ingredients are, the better your flavors. While you're not likely to have an abundance of ingredients on hand in college, if you can stock a small pantry, you'll always be just a few fresh ingredients away from a really flavorful meal.

Herbs and Spices

▲ Black pepper, ground

▲ Chili powder

▲ Cumin, ground

▲ Garlic powder

▲ Italian seasoning

▲ Oregano, dried

▲ Sea salt, fine

Beans, Grains, and Flours

▲ Beans, dried or canned

▲ Bread crumbs

▲ Cornstarch

▲ Flour, all-purpose

▲ Oats, steel-cut

▲ Pasta, dried

▲ Rice, dried

Oils, Sauces, and Other

▲ Bouillon powder or cubes

▲ Olive oil

▲ Pasta sauce

▲ Soy sauce

▲ Sugar, brown

▲ Sugar, granulated (white)

▲ Vanilla extract

▲ Worcestershire sauce

10 INSTANT POT® USAGE TIPS

The Instant Pot® is a wonderful appliance, but there can be a learning curve. Here's my best advice for proper use every time:

1. Always make sure that the exterior of your inner cooking pot is dry before placing it in the Instant Pot®.

2. Unless the recipe says to insert the trivet or steamer basket, remove it before cooking.

3. Never fill your inner cooking pot more than two-thirds full. There is a "MAX" line on the inside to use as a guide. For foods that tend to sputter and spew (beans, or some soups), fill the pot no more than half full.

4. Before using any of the pressure cooking features, be sure to set the valve to the "sealing" position. This is what keeps the steam inside and allows the pot to build up pressure.

5. Each time you prepare a recipe, be sure to add the required amount of liquid so that the pressure can build and cook the food.

6. Never place anything (like a dishtowel or pot holder) over the pressure release valve while cooking.

7. If the lid seems to stick or is hard to turn, it may mean that there is still pressure inside the cooker, and further cooling or release of pressure is required. Do not attempt to force the lid off.

8. When doing a quick release of pressure, turn the valve slowly to release the pressure a little at a time, rather than all at once.

9. Always unplug your Instant Pot® when not in use and wash it according to the instruction manual.

10. When putting away the unit, store it with the lid upside down on top of the pot to keep the cooker and the sealing ring fresh.

FREQUENTLY ASKED QUESTIONS

If you are new to cooking with an Instant Pot® or any electric pressure cooker, many of these questions are likely to come up for you as you begin exploring this new cooking appliance.

▲ The recipes list the prep time, sometimes the sauté time, the pressure cooking time, release time, and then the "total time." What is the total time?

When you use a pressure cooker, you have to account for the time the pot takes to come up to pressure before the cooking program begins its countdown. If you set your pot to pressure cook on High for 20 minutes, the clock will not start counting down those 20 minutes of cooking time until the pot has reached full pressure, which usually takes about 10 minutes, though it can be longer or shorter depending on the size of the pot and how much you put in it.

For the recipes in this book, we have listed the time it will take for you to prepare the ingredients, the time needed to sauté ingredients before pressure cooking (if necessary), the actual pressure cooking time, and, when appropriate, the time for a natural release of pressure. To get the total time for each recipe, we add up these numbers and add 10 minutes to account for the time it takes the pot to come to pressure. This should give you a good estimate of how long the dish will take you to prepare from start to finish.

▲ How much liquid do I need to use in every recipe?

The Instant Pot® needs at least 1 cup of liquid in order to create steam to build and maintain pressure. With foods that absorb liquid (such as rice) you'll need more liquid than for other foods. When cooking foods that release moisture, such as vegetables, you'll need less liquid.

▲ Steam is escaping from my Instant Pot®; is this normal?

The pressure release valve is designed to let out steam. It's normal to hear it sputter as the pot comes to pressure. If it continues to sputter, check to make sure you have your valve set to the "sealing" position. If it is, check that your sealing ring is in place and properly attached.

▲ What if I cook something and it isn't cooked all the way through—can I put it back in the Instant Pot® for more time?

Absolutely. Keep in mind that the Instant Pot® will have to come to pressure again. It won't take as long, though, because it is already warm.

▲ Is it true I shouldn't cook pasta in the Instant Pot®?

I have heard this, but I cook pasta in my Instant Pot® all the time. This being said, be picky about which pasta you cook. Lasagna,

ziti, and penne work well; very thin, delicate pasta like angel hair does not. I have shared a few recipes in this book to help you navigate cooking pasta. For best results, don't put the pasta in first, or it will stick to the inner cooking pot.

▲ If a recipe calls for chicken breasts, can I use chicken thighs instead?

Swapping thighs for breasts works well. Substitute it pound for pound and increase the cooking time by 2 minutes, since dark meat has more fat than white meat and thus takes longer to cook.

▲ Can I cook meat or other ingredients from frozen or do I need to thaw them first?

The Instant Pot® is ready to cook food straight from the freezer—no defrosting required. Keep in mind that it will take longer for the pot to come up to pressure, as the frozen food will need to thaw in the pot before it can build up enough steam. It may even take twice as long, depending on how much meat you're cooking. The recipe cooking time will remain the same, though; it's just the pressurizing process that will take longer.

You can also store leftovers in the freezer and reheat them from frozen in the Instant Pot®.

▲ Why does the sealing ring begin to smell like the food I've cooked after a few uses, and what can I do about it?

The silicone that the gasket is made of does absorb odors. This is unavoidable. You can wash it with hot, soapy water and leave the ring separate from the lid for storage so that it has a chance to air out. Another method you can try is putting 2 cups of distilled white vinegar in the inner cooking pot, attaching the lid with the sealing ring in place, and running the pot on Steam for 3 minutes; then remove the lid and ring and let the ring air-dry. You might even try letting the ring dry outside in the sunshine.

Even with these methods, you may not be able to remove the odors of previous dishes, but the good news is that this will not affect the flavor of your future dishes.

▲ What is a sling and how do I use one with my Instant Pot®?

A sling is a long strip, usually made of aluminum foil, that can be used to lower pans into the pot and/or lift them out of the pot when using the pot-in-pot method. You can also fashion a sling by cutting a silicone baking sheet into 3-inch-wide strips or using silicone rubber bands (Grifiti Bands is a popular brand).

To make a foil sling, tear off a piece of (ideally heavy-duty) aluminum foil that is at least 9 inches wide and 13 inches long. Fold the aluminum foil lengthwise into thirds. You should have a long, triple-layer strip of aluminum foil. To use, place the dish you want to put into the inner cooking pot in the center of the foil sling. Lower it into your Instant Pot®, using the ends of the sling as handles. Fold the excess foil across the top of the pan so it doesn't interfere with the lid, then cook the dish as directed in the recipe method. To lift the dish out of the pan, use the ends of the foil sling again like handles to lift it.

THIS BOOK'S RECIPES

This cookbook is a collection of favorite family recipes and otherwise popular recipes for the long days and nights of college. I realize that not all students are able to make it home for the holidays, so you'll also find recipes for a number of Thanksgiving dishes to help you enjoy holiday staples with friends or roommates when you can't travel home.

I've made a point to use familiar, easy-to-access ingredients and to make recipe prep as minimal as possible. I also tried to limit the number of ingredients called for in each recipe, so there's a good likelihood you can pull most of them off with limited shopping. Lots of recipe tips offer ingredient substitutions so you'll know what else you can use if you don't have all the called-for ingredients. Recipe labels will tell you if the ingredients are dairy-free, gluten-free, vegetarian, or vegan.

Ultimately, I hope this book—along with your Instant Pot®—serves you well throughout your years in college and beyond.

Fluffy Egg Bites (page 29)

CHAPTER 2

Breakfast

HARD- AND SOFT-BOILED EGGS

Prep time: 2 MINUTES, PLUS 5 MINUTES TO REST   *Pressure cook:* 3 MINUTES (SOFT-BOILED)
OR 5 MINUTES (HARD-BOILED) ON HIGH   *Release:* NATURAL FOR 3 TO 5 MINUTES
Total time: 23 TO 27 MINUTES

**MAKES 1 OR MORE EGGS
(YOUR CHOICE)**

**DAIRY-FREE
GLUTEN-FREE
VEGETARIAN**

EQUIPMENT
Measuring cup, trivet, large
bowl, slotted spoon

1 cup water, for steaming

1 or more large eggs

Boiling eggs is not hard but with the Instant Pot®, it's a truly
set-it-and-forget-it process. You can put just one egg in the
pot or a dozen, it doesn't make a difference—you won't need
to adjust the water or the cooking time. They come out perfect
every time and they peel easily. The key is the process. For
hard-boiled eggs, my family prefers the 5-5-5 process:
5 minutes on Manual or Pressure Cook, 5 minutes natural
pressure release, and 5 minutes to stop the cooking in ice
water. With this method, the white is just set with a thick yolk.
For soft-boiled, we use the 3-3-3 method—3 minutes instead
of 5 for each step.

1. **PLACE THE EGGS IN THE INNER COOKING POT.** Pour the water
into the inner cooking pot and place a trivet on the bottom.
Place the eggs on the trivet. It's okay if they touch, and you
can even stack them.

2. **PRESSURE COOK THE EGGS.** Lock the lid into place and turn
the valve to "sealing." Select Manual or Pressure Cook and
adjust the pressure to High. Set the time for 3 minutes for
soft-boiled eggs or 5 minutes for hard-boiled eggs. When
cooking ends, let the pressure release naturally for 3 minutes
for soft-boiled eggs, or 5 minutes for hard-boiled eggs, then
turn the valve to "venting" to quick release the remaining
pressure.

3. **PREPARE THE ICE BATH.** While the eggs cook, fill a large
bowl with ice and cold water.

The Instant Pot® College Cookbook

4. COOL THE EGGS. Unlock and remove the lid. With a slotted spoon, transfer the eggs to the ice bath. This will stop the cooking. Allow the eggs to rest in the ice bath for 5 minutes.

5. FINISH THE EGGS. Once the eggs have cooled, you can peel and eat them immediately, or store them whole in the refrigerator. Hard-boiled eggs will keep for up to 4 days. Soft-boiled eggs will keep for up to 2 days.

Appliance tip:

If you happen to have an Instant Pot® model with an Egg setting, try it out. Simply place your eggs on the trivet, as instructed, and select the Egg function. It automatically cooks for 5 minutes at high pressure, which will give you hard-boiled eggs if you make no adjustments. Manually adjust the cooking time down for soft-boiled eggs.

STEEL-CUT OATS

Prep time: 5 MINUTES   *Pressure cook:* 10 MINUTES ON HIGH   *Release:* NATURAL FOR 15 MINUTES   *Total time:* 40 MINUTES

SERVES 4

VEGETARIAN

EQUIPMENT
Measuring cups and spoons, chef's knife, mixing spoon

1 cup steel-cut oats

½ cup unsweetened applesauce

1 teaspoon ground cinnamon

½ teaspoon ground nutmeg

¼ teaspoon fine sea salt

3 cups water

1 apple, peeled, cored, and chopped

Milk, as needed

Forty minutes may seem like a long time to wait for breakfast when you could just stir some boiling water into a packet of instant oatmeal, but the from-scratch version is worth the extra wait (which is entirely hands-off time). Steel-cut oats are ultra-nutritious and an excellent source of protein, which will keep you from getting overly hungry throughout the day.

1. **PREPARE THE OATS.** Combine the oats, applesauce, cinnamon, nutmeg, salt, and water in the inner cooking pot. Stir the ingredients.

2. **PRESSURE COOK.** Lock the lid into place and turn the valve to "sealing." Select Manual or Pressure Cook and adjust the pressure to High. Set the time for 10 minutes. When cooking ends, let the pressure release naturally for 15 minutes.

3. **FINISH THE OATS.** Unlock and remove the lid. Stir the oats, then add the apple. Add milk until you reach your desired consistency. Enjoy with your favorite toppings (see tip).

Variation tip:

Try topping the oatmeal with raisins, chopped nuts, additional apples, or other fruits. You can experiment with different types of fruit (pears, peaches, bananas, berries, or any other fruit you like).

Simplify it!

Make a big batch and store leftovers in single-serving glass or BPA-free plastic containers in the refrigerator. Pop one in the microwave for a minute or two for a quick grab-and-go breakfast.

OATMEAL

Prep time: 2 MINUTES   *Pressure cook:* 4 MINUTES ON MEDIUM   *Release:* QUICK
Total time: 16 MINUTES

SERVES 4

VEGETARIAN

EQUIPMENT
Measuring cups and spoons, mixing spoon

2 cups rolled oats

5 cups water

1 tablespoon unsalted butter (optional)

½ teaspoon fine sea salt (optional)

Making oatmeal in the Instant Pot® means no standing at the stove stirring. You can put it all together, read some material for class, chat with friends, or stream a show while it cooks. The previous recipe is for Steel-Cut Oats, but many people prefer the softer texture of rolled oatmeal. Everyone likes their oatmeal cooked and served a bit differently, so this is a basic recipe; consider it the foundation, or blank canvas, to create your breakfast masterpiece. You can add raw fruit and additional spices to the oats to cook at the same time, or follow the basic recipe and add your own toppings.

1. **PREPARE THE OATMEAL.** Pour the rolled oats into the inner cooking pot. Add the water, butter (if using), and salt (if using) and stir.

2. **PRESSURE COOK.** Lock the lid into place and turn the valve to "sealing." Select Manual or Pressure Cook and adjust the pressure to Medium. Set the time for 4 minutes. When cooking ends, carefully turn the valve to "venting" to quick release the pressure. Unlock and remove the lid.

Cooking tip:

You can double the ingredients and keep the cooking time the same. I usually make a double batch at the beginning of the week and store it in individual servings, allowing anyone to grab a cup of oatmeal as a snack or a grab-and-go breakfast. Just add milk to make it creamy again.

YOGURT OR GREEK YOGURT

Prep time: 5 MINUTES *Pressure cook:* 8 TO 12 HOURS ON YOGURT SETTING
Total time: 8 TO 12 HOURS

MAKES 16 (1-CUP) SERVINGS

**GLUTEN-FREE
VEGETARIAN**

EQUIPMENT
Measuring spoon, whisk,
thermometer, small
bowl, yogurt strainer or
cheesecloth (optional)

1 gallon whole milk

2 tablespoons yogurt (use
only the kind with live
cultures)

This yogurt recipe is delicious, saves money, and is part of my weekly ritual. I love that I control what goes into it. Change up the flavorings with fresh fruit, preserves, compotes, curds, granola; it's up to you! This recipe will show you how easy it is to make traditional yogurt; strain it and you have Greek yogurt. It's easy to make, but does require time and refrigeration, as well as a thermometer for measuring the temperature of the milk. This recipe calls for cheesecloth. It looks like gauze and can be purchased at the grocery store. It is used in cooking to strain cheeses and broths. A coffee filter or clean linen dishtowel can be used as a substitute.

1. **HEAT THE MILK.** Pour the milk into the inner cooking pot. Cover with the lid. Select the Yogurt setting and then press Adjust until the Instant Pot® reads "Boil." Stir and whisk the milk occasionally to get it to heat evenly. When you hear beeping, unlock and remove the lid, and use a thermometer to test the temperature. The milk needs to be between 180°F and 185°F. If it is not hot enough, press Sauté and stir constantly until the milk reaches 180°F.

2. **COOL THE MILK.** Remove the inner cooking pot and place it in a sink filled with cold water to reduce the temperature to between 95°F and 110°F. Whisk often to help cool the milk. When the milk is cool, remove the pot from the sink and dry off the outside.

3. **ADD THE CULTURE.** Put the live culture yogurt in a small bowl and add some of the warm milk mixture; whisk together. Add the yogurt mixture to the rest of the milk in the inner cooking pot.

4. **INCUBATE THE YOGURT.** Place the inner cooking pot back in the Instant Pot® and cover. The longer you set the time, the more tart the yogurt will be. For a mild yogurt, incubate it for 6 to 8 hours. For a tangier yogurt, incubate for 8 to 10 hours.

5. FINISH THE YOGURT. When the cycle ends, remove the pot, keep it covered, and place it in the refrigerator for 6 to 8 hours. Don't disturb it; just let it rest. It should be thick enough for a spoon to stand upright in it. Stop here if you want traditional yogurt; simply unlock and remove the lid.

6. STRAIN FOR GREEK YOGURT (OPTIONAL). If you want Greek yogurt, strain using a double layer of cheesecloth.

Cooking tip:

Once your milk has reached the desired temperature (step 1), check to see if a "skin" has formed on the top. If so, carefully skim this skin off and discard it. This will ensure that your yogurt ends up nice and creamy.

BANANA BREAD

Prep time: 10 MINUTES   *Pressure cook:* 50 MINUTES ON HIGH   *Release:* QUICK
Total time: 1 HOUR 10 MINUTES

SERVES 4 (8 SLICES)

VEGETARIAN

EQUIPMENT
Measuring cups and spoons, 7-inch round cake pan, medium bowl, mixing spoon, paper towels, aluminum foil, trivet, cooling rack, chef's knife

6 tablespoons unsalted butter, melted, plus extra for greasing the pan

3 very ripe bananas

1 large egg, beaten

1 teaspoon vanilla extract

½ cup granulated sugar

1 teaspoon baking soda

Pinch fine sea salt

1½ cups all-purpose flour, divided

1 cup water, for steaming

Because the Instant Pot® cooks with steam, it is ideal for making moist cake- or bread-like recipes, like this banana bread. This recipe takes me back to my childhood, when my grandmother would bake banana bread for dessert. The next morning, she'd toast it and we'd indulge in warm, homemade banana bread smothered in butter and jam for breakfast. A 7-inch round cake pan should fit in a 3-, 6-, or 8-quart Instant Pot®. Make sure your pan fits in your inner cooking pot before beginning the recipe.

1. **PREPARE THE PAN.** Grease a 7-inch round cake pan with butter.

2. **PREPARE THE BATTER.** In a medium bowl, mash the bananas with a fork. Add the butter, egg, and vanilla and mix well. Stir in the sugar, baking soda, and salt. In ½-cup increments, add the flour to the mixture. Pour the batter into the prepared pan. Place a paper towel over it, then cover tightly with aluminum foil.

3. **PRESSURE COOK.** Pour the water into the inner cooking pot and place a trivet on the bottom. Using a sling (see page 17), lower the foil-covered pan onto the trivet. Lock the lid into place and turn the valve to "sealing." Select Manual or Pressure Cook and adjust the pressure to High. Set the time for 50 minutes. When cooking ends, carefully turn the valve to "venting" to quick release the pressure.

4. COOL THE BANANA BREAD. Unlock and remove the lid. Use the sling to remove the pan from the Instant Pot®. Let it rest for 5 minutes on a cooling rack. Remove the bread from the pan and, once cool, cut into 8 slices.

Ingredient tip:

Adjust the sugar based on how ripe your bananas are. The riper your bananas, the less sugar you'll need, but use at least ¼ cup.

Prep tip:

Do not overwork your batter. Mix until just combined for best results.

BERRIES AND CREAM BREAKFAST CAKE

Prep time: 10 MINUTES   *Pressure cook:* 35 MINUTES ON HIGH
Release: NATURAL FOR 20 MINUTES   *Total time:* 1 HOUR 15 MINUTES

SERVES 8

VEGETARIAN

EQUIPMENT

Measuring cups and
spoons, 7-inch round
cake pan, medium bowl,
large bowl, electric
mixer, mixing spoon,
paper towels,
aluminum foil, trivet,
chef's knife

1 cup (2 sticks) unsalted
butter, at room
temperature, plus extra for
greasing the pan

2 cups all-purpose
flour, plus extra for
preparing the pan

2½ teaspoons
baking powder

1 teaspoon fine sea salt

¾ cup granulated sugar

1 large egg

¾ cup milk

2 cups fresh berries

1 cup water, for steaming

1 (16-ounce) container
cream cheese frosting

Before the Instant Pot®, my weekend mornings were the only
time I could carve out some time to create a breakfast cake.
Now, this can be a weekday morning treat. It's perfect with
coffee or tea.

1. **PREPARE THE PAN.** Butter and flour a 7-inch round cake pan.

2. **PREPARE THE BATTER.** Combine the flour, baking powder,
and salt in a medium mixing bowl. In a large mixing bowl, use
an electric mixer to cream together the butter, sugar, and egg.
In ½-cup increments, mix the flour mixture into the butter
mixture. Gently stir in the milk and berries. Pour the batter into
the prepared pan. Place a paper towel over it and then cover
tightly with aluminum foil.

3. **PRESSURE COOK.** Pour the water into the inner cooking pot
and place a trivet on the bottom. Using a sling (see page 17),
lower the foil-covered pan onto the trivet. Lock the lid into
place and turn the valve to "sealing." Select Manual or
Pressure Cook and adjust the pressure to High. Set the time
to 35 minutes. When cooking ends, let the pressure release
naturally.

4. **CHECK AND COOL THE CAKE.** Unlock and remove the lid.
Use the sling to remove the pan from the pot. Remove the
aluminum foil and paper towel. Using a fork, check to ensure
that the cake is done. The fork's tines should come out clean.
If not, replace the paper towel and aluminum foil and return
the pan to the pot, lock the lid back into place, and cook for
a few more minutes. Place the cake pan on a cooling rack for
10 minutes to cool. Run a knife around the edge of the cake
and then invert it onto a plate. Allow to cool completely.

5. **FROST THE CAKE.** Open the container of frosting and scoop
½ cup of it into a microwave-safe container. Microwave it for
15 seconds. Stir the frosting and drizzle over the cake, then cut
into 8 slices. Warm and drizzle more frosting, if desired.

FLUFFY EGG BITES

Prep time: 10 MINUTES   *Pressure cook:* 8 MINUTES   *Release:* NATURAL FOR 10 MINUTES
Total time: 38 MINUTES

SERVES 4

**GLUTEN-FREE
VEGETARIAN OPTION**

EQUIPMENT
Measuring cups and
spoons, silicone egg bite
molds, medium bowl,
whisk, blender (optional),
aluminum foil

¼ cup crumbled cooked
bacon or sausage (optional)

4 large eggs

¾ cup shredded Monterey
Jack cheese

½ cup small-curd
cottage cheese

¼ cup heavy cream

½ teaspoon fine sea salt

1 cup water, for steaming

The menu at America's favorite chain coffee shop (ahem, you know which one I'm talking about) does not disappoint. The cost, however, adds up quickly. By skipping the store-bought option, both you and your wallet will be full. Make a batch of these egg bites to eat throughout the week; they reheat nicely in a microwave. If you have a blender, the results are spectacular, but no one will complain if you just use a whisk.

1. PREPARE THE EGG MIXTURE. Divide the crumbled bacon or sausage (if using) between the silicone egg bite molds. In a medium mixing bowl, whisk together the eggs, shredded cheese, cottage cheese, cream, and salt. (Alternatively, you can blend these ingredients in a blender.)

2. PREPARE THE MOLDS. Divide the egg mixture between the molds. Cover the molds with aluminum foil.

3. PRESSURE COOK THE EGGS. Pour the water into the inner cooking pot and place a trivet in the bottom. Place the molds on top of the trivet. Lock the lid, select Steam, and set the time to 8 minutes. When cooking ends, let the pressure release naturally for 10 minutes, then turn the valve to "venting" to quick release the remaining pressure.

4. FINISH THE EGGS. Unlock and remove the lid. Remove the silicone molds from the pot. Allow the eggs to rest in the mold for 2 minutes before removing.

Cooking tip:

If you don't have silicone egg bite molds, you can use silicone cupcake liners.

BREAKFAST BURRITOS

Prep time: 5 MINUTES   *Pressure cook:* 35 MINUTES ON HIGH   *Release:* QUICK
Total time: 50 MINUTES

SERVES 5

VEGETARIAN OPTION

EQUIPMENT

Measuring cups and spoons, chef's knife (optional), 7-inch heat-safe bowl or pan, medium bowl, whisk, aluminum foil, trivet, mixing spoon

Nonstick cooking spray

1¼ cups frozen hash browns

½ cup diced ham (optional)

3 large eggs

2 tablespoons milk

2 tablespoons sour cream

¼ cup shredded Cheddar cheese

⅛ teaspoon fine sea salt

⅛ teaspoon ground black pepper

1 cup water, for steaming

5 flour tortillas

These breakfast burritos are packed with goodness and make a great study snack. This recipe will make the traditional handheld burrito, but you can also smother it with your favorite sauce, or turn it into a burrito bowl. You can make the filling ahead of time and then heat it up in the microwave and wrap it in a flour tortilla for an easy, on-the-go breakfast.

1. **PREPARE THE PAN.** Grease a 7-inch heat-safe bowl or pan that fits inside the inner cooking pot with nonstick cooking spray.

2. **PREPARE THE BURRITO MIXTURE.** Put the hash browns in the prepared bowl and top with the ham (if using). In a medium bowl, whisk together the eggs, milk, sour cream, cheese, salt, and pepper. Pour the egg mixture over the meat and hash browns. Cover the bowl tightly with aluminum foil.

3. **PRESSURE COOK.** Pour the water into the inner cooking pot and place a trivet on the bottom. Place the foil-covered bowl on the trivet. Lock the lid into place and turn the valve to "sealing." Select Manual or Pressure Cook and adjust the pressure to High. Set the time to 25 minutes. When cooking ends, carefully turn the valve to "venting" to quick release the pressure.

4. **FINISH COOKING.** Unlock and remove the lid. Remove the bowl from the pot. Remove the foil and stir the egg mixture, then replace the foil. Return the bowl to the pot. Lock the lid into place and turn the valve to "sealing." Select Manual or Pressure Cook and adjust the pressure to High. Set the time to 10 minutes. When cooking ends, carefully turn the valve to "venting" to quick release the pressure. Unlock and remove the lid.

5. **ASSEMBLE THE BURRITOS.** Remove the bowl from the pot and remove the foil. Stir again, then spoon the filling onto the tortillas. Wrap the tortillas around the filling, tucking in the edges.

FRENCH TOAST CASSEROLE

Prep time: 5 MINUTES, PLUS 5 MINUTES TO REST   *Pressure cook:* 15 MINUTES ON HIGH
Release: QUICK   *Total time:* 35 MINUTES

SERVES 4

VEGETARIAN

EQUIPMENT
Measuring cups and spoons, 7-inch pan, large bowl, whisk, aluminum foil

Butter or nonstick cooking spray

2 large eggs

1 cup milk

2 teaspoons vanilla extract

1 teaspoon ground cinnamon

7 bread slices (cinnamon raisin, wheat, Italian—choose your favorite), cut into 1-inch cubes

1 cup water, for steaming

Assorted toppings (butter, maple syrup, sliced fruit, chopped nuts, chocolate chips, etc.)

My children tell me that French toast is the dish that most reminds them of family breakfasts. They remember trays heaping with French toast when they hosted sleepovers or when we visited relatives. This version is almost effortless—you don't have to stand at the stove and babysit the pan.

1. PREPARE THE PAN. Grease a 7-inch pan that fits inside the inner cooking pot with the butter.

2. PREPARE THE CASSEROLE. In a large mixing bowl, whisk together the eggs, milk, vanilla, and cinnamon. Add the bread cubes to the egg mixture and mix to coat all the bread pieces with the egg mixture. Pour the bread and egg mixture into the prepared pan. Cover the pan with aluminum foil.

3. PRESSURE COOK. Pour the water into the inner cooking pot and place a trivet on the bottom. Place the foil-covered pan on top of the trivet. Lock the lid into place and turn the valve to "sealing." Select Manual or Pressure Cook and adjust the pressure to High. Set the time to 15 minutes. When cooking ends, carefully turn the valve to "venting" to quick release the pressure.

4. FINISH THE CASSEROLE. Unlock and remove the lid. Remove the pan and the foil. Let the casserole rest for 5 minutes. Top with your favorite toppings.

Variation tip:

For maple-flavored French toast, add 2 tablespoons maple syrup to the egg mixture.

SPINACH FRITTATA

Prep time: 15 MINUTES   *Sauté:* 3 MINUTES ON MEDIUM   *Pressure cook:* 25 MINUTES ON HIGH
Release: NATURAL FOR 8 MINUTES   *Total time:* 61 MINUTES

SERVES 4

GLUTEN-FREE
VEGETARIAN

EQUIPMENT

Measuring cups and spoons, chef's knife, can opener, 7-inch springform pan, aluminum foil, wooden spoon or silicone spatula, medium bowl, whisk, trivet, paper towels

Nonstick cooking spray

2 tablespoons olive oil

1 onion, chopped

2 cups baby spinach

2 garlic cloves, minced

8 large eggs

2 cups shredded mozzarella cheese, divided

1 cup canned diced tomatoes, drained (about half of a 15-ounce can)

¼ cup milk

½ teaspoon fine sea salt

¼ teaspoon ground black pepper

1 cup water, for steaming

Sour cream, for topping (optional)

A frittata is very much like an omelet. The primary difference is that the filling in a frittata is mixed in with the eggs, whereas an omelet's filling is folded in as it cooks. This frittata was my husband's first recipe request from the Instant Pot®. This is a basic recipe, and one I hope you make your own by adding your favorite meats or vegetables.

1. PREPARE THE PAN. Line a 7-inch springform pan with aluminum foil to keep the liquid from leaking, then spray the foil with nonstick cooking spray.

2. SAUTÉ THE VEGETABLES. Add the oil to the inner cooking pot. Select Sauté and adjust the heat to Medium. Once the oil is hot, add the onion, spinach, and garlic and cook, stirring, for 3 minutes, until the onion is almost translucent and the spinach is wilted. Transfer the vegetables to a medium bowl. Rinse out the inner cooking pot to make sure there's no onion or garlic that may have stuck to the bottom.

3. PREPARE THE FRITTATA. Add the eggs, 1 cup of cheese, the tomatoes, milk, salt, and pepper to the bowl and whisk until well combined. Pour the egg mixture into the prepared pan and cover with aluminum foil.

4. PRESSURE COOK. Pour the water into the inner cooking pot and place a trivet in the bottom. Using a sling (see page 17), lower the foil-covered pan onto the trivet. Lock the lid into place and turn the vale to "sealing." Select Manual or Pressure Cook and adjust the pressure to High. Set the time for 25 minutes. When cooking ends, let the pressure release naturally for 8 minutes, then turn the valve to "venting" to quick release the remaining pressure.

5. FINISH. Unlock and remove the lid. Using the sling, lift the pan out of the pot. Remove the foil. Gently dab a paper towel on top of the frittata to remove any moisture that may have built up. As the frittata cools, it will begin to pull away from the edges. Run a knife around the edges to loosen it. Place a plate over top of frittata and turn the pan upside down so that the frittata releases. Top with the remaining 1 cup of cheese and sour cream, if desired.

Cilantro-Lime Rice (page 41) and Baked Beans (page 39)

CHAPTER 3

Everyday Staples

BASIC BEANS

Prep time: 5 MINUTES *Pressure cook:* 30 MINUTES ON HIGH   *Release:* NATURAL FOR 10 MINUTES
Total time: 55 MINUTES

SERVES 6

DAIRY-FREE
GLUTEN-FREE
VEGAN

EQUIPMENT
Measuring cups
and spoons

1 pound dried beans

8 cups water

2 teaspoons fine sea salt

This basic bean recipe can be easily adapted for just about any type of dried beans. I like to make pots of beans that are simply seasoned and then use them in other dishes, like bean soup and Taco Pie (page 94), or toss them into salads. For more information about cooking beans in the Instant Pot®, see page 12.

1. PREPARE THE BEANS. Rinse the beans and discard any that float. Combine the beans, water, and salt in the inner cooking pot.

2. PRESSURE COOK. Lock the lid into place and turn the valve to "sealing." Select Manual or Pressure Cook and adjust the pressure to High. Set the time for 30 minutes. When cooking ends, let the pressure release naturally for 10 minutes, then turn the valve to "venting" to quick release the remaining pressure. Unlock and remove the lid.

Simplify it!

Make a large batch of beans and measure them into freezer-safe zip-top bags in 2-cup portions. They'll keep in the freezer for up to 6 months, and each portion can be used in place of 1 (15-ounce) can of beans.

BLACK BEANS

Prep time: 10 MINUTES   *Sauté:* 5 MINUTES ON MEDIUM   *Pressure cook:* 25 MINUTES ON HIGH
Release: NATURAL FOR 10 MINUTES   *Total time:* 1 HOUR

SERVES 4

DAIRY-FREE
GLUTEN-FREE
VEGETARIAN OPTION

EQUIPMENT

Measuring cups and spoons, chef's knife, can opener, wooden spoon or silicone spatula, small bowl

1 pound dried black beans, rinsed and sorted

1 large green bell pepper, seeded and chopped

1 medium onion, chopped

1 teaspoon dried oregano

1 bay leaf

4 ounces salt pork, cut into 1-inch pieces, or 1 ham hock (optional)

1 (14-ounce) can diced tomatoes, drained

4 cups chicken or vegetable broth

¼ cup distilled white vinegar

1 teaspoon granulated sugar

2 teaspoons fine sea salt, if not using the pork or ham hock

You can eat these beans on their own, mix them with rice to make *morros*, simmer them until no longer soupy and serve as a black bean dip, or make black bean burgers! The *sofrito*—a sautéed mixture of onions and peppers—is optional, but it adds a ton of flavor to the beans. See the tip for how to make it.

1. PREPARE THE BEANS. Rinse the beans and discard any that float. Combine the beans, bell pepper, onion, oregano, bay leaf, pork (if using), tomatoes, and broth in the inner cooking pot. The liquid should cover the beans by about 1½ inches. Add water, if needed, to achieve this.

2. PRESSURE COOK. Lock the lid into place and turn the valve to "sealing." Select Manual or Pressure Cook and adjust the pressure to High. Set the time for 25 minutes. When cooking ends, let the pressure release naturally for 10 minutes, then turn the valve to "venting" to quick release the remaining pressure.

3. FINISH THE BEANS. Unlock and remove the lid and taste the beans for doneness (see tip). If done, use a fork to press the beans against the side of the pot to mash them. This will thicken the liquid. Stir in the vinegar, sugar, salt (if not using pork or ham), and the reserved sofrito (if using).

Cooking tip:

To make the sofrito, do it before the first step of the recipe. Add 3 tablespoons olive oil to the inner cooking pot. Select Sauté and adjust the heat to Medium. When the oil is hot, add 1 cup of green bell pepper strips, ½ cup of sliced onions, and 1 garlic clove, minced. Sauté until the vegetables are tender, 5 minutes. Transfer the sofrito to a small bowl, then follow the remaining instructions as written.

PINTO BEANS

Prep time: 5 MINUTES   *Sauté:* 5 MINUTES ON MEDIUM   *Pressure cook:* 45 MINUTES ON HIGH
Release: NATURAL FOR 30 MINUTES   *Total time:* 1 HOUR 35 MINUTES

SERVES 6

DAIRY-FREE
GLUTEN-FREE
VEGETARIAN OPTION

EQUIPMENT
Measuring cups and
spoons, chef's knife,
wooden spoon or
silicone spatula

8 bacon slices, cut into
small pieces (optional)

1 tablespoon olive oil,
if not using bacon

1 onion, finely chopped

1 garlic clove, minced

1 pound dry pinto beans

4 cups beef, chicken,
or vegetable broth

½ teaspoon ground cumin

1 teaspoon fine sea salt

½ teaspoon ground
black pepper

Pinto beans make for a delicious side dish or soup. We add
them to our Tex-Mex Chili (page 57) and use them to make
refried beans (see the tip). I like to top these with shredded
cheese, chopped onion, and sour cream.

1. **SAUTÉ THE VEGETABLES.** Combine the bacon or oil, onion,
and garlic in the inner cooking pot. Select Sauté and adjust
the heat to Medium. Sauté, stirring occasionally, for 5 minutes.

2. **PREPARE THE BEANS.** Rinse the beans and discard any that
float. Add the beans, broth, cumin, salt, and pepper to the pot
and stir well.

3. **PRESSURE COOK.** Lock the lid into place and turn the valve
to "sealing." Select Manual or Pressure Cook and adjust the
pressure to High. Set the time for 45 minutes. When cooking
ends, let the pressure release naturally for 30 minutes, then
turn the valve to "venting" to quick release the remaining
pressure. Unlock and remove the lid.

> ### Variation tip:
>
> To make refried beans, combine 4 cups of the cooked
> pinto beans and ½ cup of the cooking liquid in the inner
> cooking pot. Select Pressure cook and adjust the pres-
> sure to High. Set the time for 3 minutes. When cooking
> ends, carefully turn the valve to "venting" to quick
> release the pressure. Unlock and remove the lid. Using
> a fork or potato masher, mash the beans until they're
> creamy in consistency. Refried beans work well as a
> side dish or can be spread on tortillas and sprinkled with
> grated cheese for a speedy bean and cheese burrito.
> You can also use them in my Taco Pie (page 94).

BAKED BEANS

Prep time: 5 MINUTES   *Sauté:* 6 MINUTES ON MEDIUM   *Pressure cook:* 8 MINUTES ON HIGH
Release: NATURAL FOR 15 MINUTES   *Total time:* 44 MINUTES

SERVES 8

DAIRY-FREE
VEGETARIAN OPTION

EQUIPMENT

Measuring cups and spoons, chef's knife, can opener, wooden spoon or silicone spatula, paper towels, mixing spoon

4 bacon slices (optional)

1 (15-ounce) can kidney beans, rinsed and drained

1 (15-ounce) can pinto beans, rinsed and drained

1 (15-ounce) can great northern beans, rinsed and drained

¾ cup water

½ cup ketchup

⅓ cup brown sugar (not packed)

1 tablespoon ground mustard

1 teaspoon chili powder

This is my go-to recipe for baked beans that are sweet, rich, and tangy with a kick of spice. Their creamy texture makes them a perfect side dish, whether you eat them hot or cold.

1. SAUTÉ THE BACON. Add the bacon (if using) to the inner cooking pot. Select Sauté and adjust the heat to Medium. Cook the bacon for 3 minutes on each side, until almost crisp. Transfer the bacon to a paper towel—lined plate to drain, then chop it into bite-size pieces. Drain the fat from the pot.

2. PRESSURE COOK. Return the bacon to the pot and add the kidney beans, pinto beans, great northern beans, water, ketchup, sugar, mustard, and chili powder. Lock the lid into place and turn the valve to "sealing." Select Manual or Pressure Cook and adjust the pressure to High. Set the time for 8 minutes. When cooking ends, let the pressure release naturally for 15 minutes, then turn the valve to "venting" to quick release the remaining pressure. Unlock and remove the lid and stir well before serving.

Ingredient tip:

You can substitute 2 cups of Instant Pot®—cooked beans (page 36) for each of the cans of beans listed.

BASIC WHITE RICE

Prep time: 2 MINUTES *Pressure cook:* RICE SETTING (ABOUT 12 MINUTES)
Release: NATURAL FOR 10 MINUTES *Total time:* 34 MINUTES

SERVES 6

DAIRY-FREE
GLUTEN-FREE
VEGAN

EQUIPMENT

Measuring cups and
spoons, mixing spoon

1 cup long-grain white rice

1 cup water

1 teaspoon vegetable oil

Pinch fine sea salt

Basic white rice goes with just about everything and my kids
eat it by the potful. You can use this recipe to cook other types
of rice (brown, basmati, jasmine, etc.), but you may need to
adjust the cooking time. For more information about cooking
rice in the Instant Pot®, see page 13.

1. **PREPARE THE RICE.** Rinse the rice under cold running water
until the water runs clear. Drain. Combine the rice, water, oil,
and salt in the inner cooking pot and stir.

2. **PRESSURE COOK.** Lock the lid into place and turn the valve
to "sealing." Select Rice. The pot will automatically set to the
time needed for white rice. From experience, this recipe cooks
for 12 minutes under pressure. When cooking ends, let the
pressure release naturally for 10 minutes, then turn the valve
to "venting" to quick release the remaining pressure.

3. **FLUFF THE RICE.** Unlock and remove the lid and use a fork to
fluff the rice.

Variation tip:

Make pineapple rice by stirring ½ cup diced pineapple,
well drained, into the rice after cooking. Add ½ cup
diced ham to turn it into a quick meal.

CILANTRO-LIME RICE

Prep time: 10 MINUTES, PLUS 4 MINUTES TO REST   *Sauté:* 1 MINUTE ON MEDIUM
Pressure cook: 7 MINUTES ON HIGH   *Release:* QUICK   *Total time:* 32 MINUTES

SERVES 4

DAIRY-FREE
GLUTEN-FREE
VEGAN OPTION

EQUIPMENT
Measuring cups and spoons, mixing spoon

2 tablespoons olive oil

1 cup long-grain white rice

1 garlic clove, minced

1¼ cups low-sodium chicken or vegetable broth, or water

¼ teaspoon fine sea salt (½ teaspoon if using water instead of broth)

¼ cup chopped fresh cilantro

½ teaspoon grated lime zest (optional)

2 teaspoons freshly squeezed lime juice

A wildly popular dish at Chipotle restaurants, cilantro-lime rice is easy to make at home, and with an Instant Pot®, it's as quick as it is tasty. If you don't have fresh cilantro, look for cilantro paste in the produce or frozen section of your supermarket.

1. SAUTÉ THE RICE. Select Sauté and adjust to heat to Medium. Add the oil to the inner cooking pot. When it shimmers and flows easily, add the rice and garlic and stir to coat the rice with the oil, cooking for about 1 minute, or until the garlic is fragrant. Add the broth and salt.

2. PRESSURE COOK. Lock the lid into place and turn the valve to "sealing." Select Pressure Cook or Manual and adjust the pressure to High. Set the time for 7 minutes. When cooking ends, carefully turn the valve to "venting" to quick release the pressure.

3. FINISH THE RICE. Unlock and remove the lid. Add the cilantro, lime zest (if using), and lime juice. Stir very gently to combine. Put the lid back on the pot but do not lock it into place. Let the rice sit for 3 to 4 minutes. Fluff with a fork.

COCONUT RICE

Prep time: 10 MINUTES, PLUS 4 MINUTES TO REST   *Pressure cook:* 7 MINUTES ON HIGH
Release: QUICK   *Total time:* 31 MINUTES

SERVES 4

DAIRY-FREE
GLUTEN-FREE
VEGAN

EQUIPMENT
Measuring cups and
spoons, can opener,
mixing spoon

1 cup basmati or long-grain
white rice, rinsed
and drained

¾ cup canned
coconut milk

½ cup water

½ teaspoon fine sea salt

3 tablespoons toasted
shredded unsweetened
coconut (optional)

Creamy coconut rice goes well with a variety of Asian-inspired dishes, and it's also great with grilled or roasted meats. For a more substantial side dish, stir in thawed frozen green peas and cooked mushrooms along with the toasted coconut.

1. **PREPARE THE INGREDIENTS.** Combine the rice, coconut milk, water, and salt in the inner cooking pot. Stir to combine.

2. **PRESSURE COOK.** Lock the lid into place. Select Pressure Cook or Manual and adjust the pressure to High. Set the time for 7 minutes. When cooking ends, carefully turn the valve to "venting" to quick release the pressure.

3. **FINISH THE RICE.** Unlock and remove the lid. Gently stir in the toasted coconut (if using). Put the lid back on the pot but do not lock it into place. Let the rice sit for 3 to 4 minutes. Fluff with a fork.

Ingredient tip:

You may be able to buy toasted shredded coconut, but if not, you can toast it right in the Instant Pot® before starting the rice. Select Sauté and adjust the heat to Low. Add the coconut and cook, stirring constantly, for 2 to 3 minutes, until the coconut is light golden brown and fragrant.

SPANISH RICE

Prep time: 5 MINUTES   *Sauté:* 5 MINUTES ON MEDIUM   *Pressure cook:* 10 MINUTES ON HIGH
Release: NATURAL FOR 10 MINUTES   *Total time:* 40 MINUTES

SERVES 6

GLUTEN-FREE
VEGETARIAN

EQUIPMENT
Measuring cups and
spoons, chef's knife,
wooden spoon or
silicone spatula

2 tablespoons olive oil

1 small onion,
finely chopped

1 green bell pepper, seeded
and chopped (optional)

2 large celery stalks, diced
(optional)

2 cups hot water

2 cups long-grain
white rice

2 tomatoes, peeled,
seeded, and chopped

1 teaspoon fine sea salt

½ teaspoon chili powder

1 cup shredded Monterey
Jack or Cheddar cheese

This easy recipe is the perfect side to complement your
favorite Mexican dishes, like Taco Pie (page 94) or refried
beans (see the tip on page 38), or simply add some protein
for a tasty, satisfying rice bowl.

1. PREPARE THE VEGETABLES AND RICE. Select Sauté and
adjust the heat to Medium. Add the oil and heat until shim-
mering. Add the onion, bell pepper, and celery and sauté for
5 minutes. Pour in the water and stir in the rice, tomatoes, salt,
and chili powder. Bring to a boil.

2. PRESSURE COOK. Lock the lid into place and turn the valve
to "sealing." Select Manual or Pressure Cook and adjust the
pressure to High. Set the time for 10 minutes. When cooking
ends, let the pressure release naturally for 10 minutes, then
turn the valve to "venting" to quick release the remaining
pressure.

3. FINISH THE RICE. Unlock and remove the lid and use a fork
to fluff the rice. Stir in the cheese.

Zuppa Toscana (page 54)

Soups and Stews

CREAMY TOMATO SOUP

Prep time: 5 MINUTES *Sauté:* 5 MINUTES ON MEDIUM *Pressure cook:* 7 MINUTES ON HIGH
Release: QUICK *Total time:* 27 MINUTES

SERVES 4

GLUTEN-FREE OPTION
VEGETARIAN OPTION

EQUIPMENT
Measuring cups and spoons, chef's knife, can opener

1 tablespoon unsalted butter

½ small onion, diced

2 (28-ounce) cans crushed tomatoes

2 tablespoons granulated sugar

1 cup low-sodium chicken or vegetable broth

1 teaspoon Worcestershire sauce (optional)

½ cup heavy cream

Chopped fresh basil, for garnish

My children who are in college make this soup when they're missing home. It's a longtime favorite at our house. We like it paired with crisp grilled cheese sandwiches. When my children were smaller, I would use a candy mold to shape white rice into a heart to garnish the center of the bowl of soup.

1. **BEGIN THE SOUP.** Select Sauté and adjust the heat to Medium. Add the butter to the inner cooking pot. When it begins to foam, add the onion and sauté for 5 minutes, until it is beginning to brown and caramelize. Add the tomatoes, sugar, broth, and Worcestershire sauce (if using), and stir to loosen any pieces of onion that may have stuck to the pot.

2. **PRESSURE COOK.** Lock the lid into place and turn the valve to "sealing." Select Manual or Pressure Cook and adjust the pressure to High. Set the time for 7 minutes. When cooking ends, carefully turn the valve to "venting" to quick release the pressure.

3. **FINISH THE SOUP.** Unlock and remove the lid and stir in the cream. Let warm through and garnish with the basil.

Ingredient tip:

Worcestershire sauce is made from anchovies. Most store-bought Worcestershire sauces are not gluten-free, but the one from Lea & Perrins is a gluten-free option. If you don't have Worcestershire sauce or prefer a vegetarian substitution, for every tablespoon of Worcestershire sauce called for in a recipe mix together 2 teaspoons soy sauce, ¼ teaspoon lemon juice, ¼ teaspoon granulated sugar, and ¼ teaspoon hot pepper sauce.

QUICK LENTIL TOMATO SOUP

Prep time: 5 MINUTES   *Pressure cook:* 12 MINUTES ON HIGH   *Release:* NATURAL FOR
10 MINUTES   *Total time:* 37 MINUTES

SERVES 4

DAIRY-FREE
GLUTEN-FREE
VEGAN OPTION

EQUIPMENT
Measuring cups and
spoons, can opener,
small bowl

2 teaspoons cornstarch

6 cups plus 4 teaspoons
cold water, divided

1 cup dried lentils

1 (28-ounce) can diced
tomatoes, drained

1 chicken or vegetable
bouillon cube (optional)

1 tablespoon onion powder

2 teaspoons brown sugar
(optional)

1 teaspoon fine sea salt

¼ teaspoon ground
black pepper

Chopped fresh basil,
for garnish

This easy soup is made of ingredients that you likely already
have in your cabinets. The delicious flavors will warm you
up and brighten your mood. This light tomato soup base
combines with hearty lentils to make it a substantial meal.
During my college years, I was a nanny for a family that made
a variation of this soup for Lent and other fasting days.

1. PREPARE THE INGREDIENTS. In a small bowl, make a slurry by
stirring together the cornstarch and 4 teaspoons of cold water
until smooth. Combine the lentils, tomatoes, 6 cups of water,
slurry, bouillon (if using), onion powder, brown sugar (if using),
salt, and pepper in the inner cooking pot.

2. PRESSURE COOK. Lock the lid into place and turn the valve
to "sealing." Select Manual or Pressure Cook and adjust the
pressure to High. Set the time for 12 minutes. When cooking
ends, let the pressure release naturally for 10 minutes, then
turn the valve to "venting" to quick release the remaining
pressure.

3. FINISH THE SOUP. Unlock and remove the lid. Stir the soup,
taste, and adjust the seasoning as needed. Stir in the basil.

BROCCOLI AND CHEESE SOUP

Prep time: 5 MINUTES   *Sauté:* 3 MINUTES ON MEDIUM   *Pressure cook:* 12 MINUTES ON HIGH
Release: NATURAL FOR 5 MINUTES   *Total time:* 35 MINUTES

SERVES 4

VEGETARIAN OPTION

EQUIPMENT

Measuring cups and spoons, chef's knife, can opener, wooden spoon or silicone spatula, small bowl, whisk

2 tablespoons unsalted butter

1 small onion, chopped

1 cup sliced carrots

2 (14-ounce) cans low-sodium chicken or vegetable broth

1 tablespoon all-purpose flour

1 cup milk

1 (16-ounce) package frozen chopped broccoli, thawed

1 cup half-and-half

2 cups shredded Cheddar cheese

1 teaspoon fine sea salt

½ teaspoon ground black pepper

This cheesy broccoli soup is comfort food for the soul. Crisp fall and chilly winter weather beg for the delicious combination of creamy and rich Cheddar cheese and healthy broccoli. There's no need to fight the weather; this soup is so easy to make, you can whip up a pot whenever the craving hits. This recipe is one you'll make over and over again.

1. **SAUTÉ THE VEGETABLES.** Select Sauté and adjust the heat to Medium. Add the butter to the inner cooking pot. When the butter is foaming, add the onion and carrots and sauté for 3 minutes. Add the broth.

2. **PRESSURE COOK.** Lock the lid into place and turn the valve to "sealing." Select Manual or Pressure Cook and adjust the pressure to High. Set the time for 12 minutes. When cooking ends, let the pressure release naturally for 5 minutes, then turn the valve to "venting" to quick release the remaining pressure.

3. **FINISH THE SOUP.** In a small mixing bowl, whisk the flour into the milk. Unlock and remove the lid of the pot and add the broccoli to the hot soup. Whisk in the milk and flour mixture, along with the half-and-half. Stir in the cheese until melted. Season with salt and pepper.

LASAGNA SOUP

Prep time: 5 MINUTES   *Sauté:* 5 MINUTES ON MEDIUM   *Pressure cook:* 4 MINUTES ON HIGH
Release: NATURAL FOR 10 MINUTES   *Total time:* 34 MINUTES

SERVES 8

EQUIPMENT

Measuring cups and spoons, chef's knife, wooden spoon or silicone spatula

1 tablespoon unsalted butter

1 small onion, chopped

1 tablespoon minced garlic

1 green bell pepper, seeded and chopped (optional)

1 pound Italian sausage, casings removed

2 (24-ounce) jars pasta sauce

4 cups low-sodium beef broth

1 tablespoon Italian seasoning

8 ounces lasagna noodles, broken up

1 cup ricotta cheese, for serving (optional)

1 cup shredded mozzarella cheese, for serving

Traditional lasagna takes a lot of time and effort. This dish gives you all the flavors of lasagna in an easy-to-make soup. If you let it sit overnight, the noodles will absorb the sauce— you can eat it as a lasagna/goulash, or you can stir in some broth or pasta sauce and bring it back to a soupy consistency.

1. **SAUTÉ THE VEGETABLES AND SAUSAGE.** Select Sauté and adjust the heat to Medium. Add the butter to the inner cooking pot. When it is foaming, add the onion, garlic, bell pepper (if using), and sausage and sauté for 5 minutes, breaking up the sausage.

2. **ADD THE REMAINING INGREDIENTS.** Pour in the pasta sauce, broth, and Italian seasoning and stir to combine. Add the broken-up lasagna noodles and stir to coat the noodles.

3. **PRESSURE COOK.** Lock the lid into place and turn the valve to "sealing." Select Manual or Pressure Cook and adjust the pressure to High. Set the time for 4 minutes. When cooking ends, let the pressure release naturally for 10 minutes, then turn the valve to "venting" to quick release the remaining pressure.

4. **FINISH THE SOUP.** Unlock and remove the lid. Stir the soup and ladle into bowls. Garnish each serving with a dollop of ricotta cheese (if using) and a sprinkle of mozzarella.

NAVY BEAN SOUP

Prep time: 5 MINUTES   *Sauté:* 5 MINUTES ON MEDIUM   *Pressure cook:* 25 MINUTES ON HIGH
Release: NATURAL FOR 20 MINUTES   *Total time:* 1 HOUR 5 MINUTES

SERVES 4

**DAIRY-FREE
GLUTEN-FREE
VEGAN OPTION**

EQUIPMENT
Measuring cups and
spoons, chef's knife,
wooden spoon or
silicone spatula

2 tablespoons olive oil

1 cup finely chopped onion

1 cup finely chopped celery
(optional)

2 medium carrots,
finely chopped

2 garlic cloves, minced

1 pound dried navy beans

8 cups low-sodium chicken
broth or water

2 ham hocks (optional)

1 teaspoon fine sea salt

Beans are a great staple to keep in your pantry. The Instant Pot® enables you to take dried beans and turn them into a hot bowl of soup in under an hour. This is a basic bean soup that is traditionally cooked with ham hocks for flavor, but you can leave them out and use water or vegetable broth in place of chicken broth for a vegan option, if you prefer.

1. SAUTÉ THE VEGETABLES. Select Sauté and adjust the heat to Medium. Add the oil and heat until it shimmers. Add the onion, celery (if using), carrots, and garlic and sauté for 5 minutes.

2. ADD THE REMAINING INGREDIENTS. Rinse the beans and discard any that float. Add the beans, broth, ham hocks (if using), and salt and stir.

3. PRESSURE COOK. Lock the lid into place and turn the valve to "sealing." Select Manual or Pressure Cook and adjust the pressure to High. Set the time for 25 minutes. When cooking ends, let the pressure release naturally for 20 minutes, then turn the valve to "venting" to quick release the pressure.

4. FINISH THE SOUP. Unlock and remove the lid and test the beans for doneness (see tip). Use a fork to mash some of the beans against the side of the Instant Pot® to thicken the soup.

Recipe tip:

If your beans aren't cooked quite done, just put the lid back on, turn the valve to "sealing," and set the time for 5 to 10 minutes, depending on how underdone the beans are. The pot will come to pressure quickly because it's already hot. When cooking ends, carefully turn the valve to "venting" to quick release the pressure.

WISCONSIN CHEDDAR AND BRATWURST SOUP

Prep time: 5 MINUTES   *Sauté:* 10 MINUTES ON MEDIUM   *Pressure cook:* 5 MINUTES ON HIGH
Release: QUICK   *Total time:* 30 MINUTES

SERVES 8

EQUIPMENT

Measuring cups and spoons, chef's knife, can opener, wooden spoon or silicone spatula

4 tablespoons (½ stick) unsalted butter

1 (28-ounce) bag frozen potatoes O'Brien

1 celery stalk, chopped (optional)

2 carrots, chopped

¼ cup all-purpose flour

2 (14-ounce) cans low-sodium chicken broth

1 tablespoon Dijon mustard

½ small head cabbage, shredded (optional)

1 pound smoked sausage, cut into bite-size pieces

2 cups milk or half-and-half

2 cups shredded sharp Cheddar cheese

Dinner night with Kellie, my best friend from high school, and her husband, Mike, is something we always look forward to. Mike is an amazing cook and introduced me to this delicious soup. It's a meal all by itself. It's quick, easy, and a great way to warm up on a cold day.

1. SAUTÉ THE VEGETABLES. Select Sauté and adjust the heat to Medium. Add the butter to the inner cooking pot and heat until it foams. Add the potatoes, celery (if using), and carrots and sauté for 5 minutes.

2. PREPARE THE SOUP BASE. Add the flour to the vegetables and stir constantly until the vegetables are coated. Slowly add the broth, stirring constantly to blend the roux into the broth. Add the mustard and stir to get out any lumps. Add the cabbage (if using) and sausage.

3. PRESSURE COOK. Lock the lid into place and turn the valve to "sealing." Select Manual or Pressure Cook and adjust the heat to High. Set the time for 5 minutes. When cooking ends, carefully turn the valve to "venting" to quick release the pressure.

4. FINISH THE SOUP. Unlock and remove the lid and stir the milk into the soup. Add the cheese and stir until it melts.

CHICKEN ENCHILADA SOUP

Prep time: 5 MINUTES   *Pressure cook:* 5 MINUTES ON HIGH   *Release:* NATURAL FOR 10 MINUTES
Total time: 30 MINUTES

SERVES 4

EQUIPMENT
Measuring cups and spoons, chef's knife, mixing spoon, can opener, small bowl

2 boneless, skinless chicken breasts

1 (15-ounce) can kidney beans, rinsed and drained

1 (14-ounce) can diced tomatoes, drained

1 (14-ounce) can sweet corn kernels, drained

1 small onion, chopped

1 green bell pepper, seeded, and diced (optional)

1 jalapeño, seeded and diced (optional)

1 (10-ounce) can enchilada sauce

½ cup low-sodium chicken broth

1½ cups milk

3 tablespoons cornstarch

3 tablespoons cold water

I love Mexican cuisine, especially chicken enchiladas. This soup captures all of those flavors in an easy and delicious bowl—shredded chicken breast, kidney beans, tomatoes, and sweet corn all smothered in an enchilada sauce thinned with chicken broth. Garnish this soup with shredded cheese, sour cream, sliced avocado, tortilla strips, additional jalapeños, or olives—it's all up to you!

1. **PREPARE THE SOUP.** Combine the chicken, beans, tomatoes, corn, onion, peppers (if using), enchilada sauce, and broth in the inner cooking pot.

2. **PRESSURE COOK.** Lock the lid into place and turn the valve to "sealing." Select Manual or Pressure Cook and select High. Set the time for 5 minutes. When cooking ends, let the pressure release naturally for 10 minutes, then turn the valve to "venting" to quick release the remaining pressure.

3. **FINISH THE SOUP.** Unlock and remove the lid. Transfer the chicken to a cutting board or plate. Shred using two forks or cut into bite-size pieces. Return the chicken to the pot, add the milk, and stir. Make a slurry by stirring together the cornstarch and cold water in a small bowl until smooth. Stir the slurry into the soup, stirring until the broth thickens slightly.

BASIC BEEF STEW

Prep time: 10 MINUTES   *Sauté:* 7 MINUTES ON HIGH   *Pressure cook:* 38 MINUTES ON HIGH
Release: QUICK   *Total time:* 1 HOUR 5 MINUTES

SERVES 4

EQUIPMENT

Measuring cups and spoons, chef's knife, medium bowl

1½ pounds beef stew meat

¼ cup all-purpose flour

2 tablespoons vegetable oil

6 cups low-sodium beef broth

1 large onion, cut into 8 wedges

8 carrots, cut into 1-inch pieces

4 potatoes, scrubbed or peeled, cut into 1-inch chunks

3 celery stalks, cut into 1-inch pieces

½ teaspoon fine sea salt

¼ teaspoon ground black pepper

Beef stew is the perfect all-in-one meal. Showcasing tender, moist stew meat, perfectly cooked potatoes, and vegetables all smothered in rich, hearty broth, this recipe is sure to become your go-to.

1. PREPARE THE BEEF. In a medium mixing bowl, toss the stew meat with the flour until coated.

2. BROWN THE BEEF. Select Sauté and adjust the heat to High. Add the oil to the inner cooking pot. Add about half of the meat to the oil and brown (the longer you brown the meat, the darker your sauce will be). Transfer the browned beef to a plate and repeat with the remaining meat. Add the broth and onion and return the first batch of beef to the pot.

3. PRESSURE COOK THE BEEF. Lock the lid into place and turn the valve to "sealing." Select Manual or Pressure Cook and adjust the pressure to High. Set the time for 30 minutes. When cooking ends, turn the valve to "venting" to quick release the pressure.

4. ADD THE REMAINING INGREDIENTS. Unlock and remove the lid. Add the carrots, potatoes, celery, salt, and pepper.

5. PRESSURE COOK. Lock the lid into place and turn the valve to "sealing." Select Manual or Pressure Cook and adjust the pressure to High. Set the time for 8 minutes. When cooking ends, carefully turn the valve to "venting" to quick release the pressure. Unlock and remove the lid.

ZUPPA TOSCANA

Prep time: 5 MINUTES *Sauté:* 5 MINUTES ON MEDIUM *Pressure cook:* 15 MINUTES ON HIGH
Release: QUICK *Total time:* 35 MINUTES

SERVES 4

**<30 MINUTES
GLUTEN-FREE**

EQUIPMENT
Measuring cups and
spoons, chef's knife, can
opener, wooden spoon or
silicone spatula

1 tablespoon olive oil

1 cup chopped onion

1 pound Italian sausage,
casings removed

2 garlic cloves, minced

¼ to ½ teaspoon red
pepper flakes

1 (14-ounce) can
low-sodium chicken broth

2 large russet potatoes,
halved and cut into
¼-inch-thick slices

4 cups water

2 cups chopped kale

Fine sea salt

Ground black pepper

1 cup heavy cream

6 bacon slices, cooked and
cut into bite-size pieces

Zuppa Toscana translates to "soup in the style of Tuscany,"
though the addition of cream makes this an Americanized
version. I used to make it over the stove, but seriously, who
can wait that long? I don't regret the time I used to put into it;
it's how I perfected this recipe. This soup is loaded with spicy
Italian sausage, fresh kale, and russet potatoes in a creamy
broth, and with the Instant Pot®, it's super easy to make.
Everyone loves it, so you'll want to stock up.

1. **SAUTÉ THE VEGETABLES.** Select Sauté and adjust the heat
to Medium. Add the oil to the inner cooking pot. When hot,
add the onion and sausage and sauté for 5 minutes, breaking
up the sausage. Add the garlic and red pepper flakes and stir.

2. **ADD THE REMAINING INGREDIENTS.** Add the chicken broth
and stir to release any onion pieces that may have stuck to
the bottom. Stir in the potatoes and water. Scatter the kale
on top of the liquid in the pot. Season with salt and pepper.

3. **PRESSURE COOK.** Lock the lid into place and turn the valve
to "sealing." Select Manual or Pressure Cook and adjust the
pressure to High. Set the time for 15 minutes. When cooking
ends, carefully turn the valve to "venting" to quick release
the pressure.

4. FINISH THE SOUP. Unlock and remove the lid and stir in the cream. Heat through, then stir in the bacon.

Recipe tip:

You can make this soup ahead of time, omitting the cream, and freeze it. Then, simply defrost the soup in the refrigerator overnight or in the microwave. Heat the soup and stir in the cream just before serving.

Ingredient tip:

When you take out pizza, set aside those little packets of red pepper flakes. You can use them in recipes like this one.

SPANISH CHILI

Prep time: 5 MINUTES   *Sauté:* 5 MINUTES ON HIGH   *Pressure cook:* 15 MINUTES ON HIGH
Release: QUICK   *Total time:* 3 MINUTES

SERVES 6

DAIRY-FREE
GLUTEN-FREE

EQUIPMENT
Measuring cups and spoons, chef's knife, can opener, wooden spoon or silicone spatula

1 tablespoon vegetable oil

1 pound lean ground beef

2 onions, chopped

2 garlic cloves, minced

2 (16-ounce) cans kidney beans, rinsed and drained

1 (14-ounce) can tomato purée

1 (14-ounce) can stewed tomatoes, drained

2 tablespoons chili powder

½ teaspoon fine sea salt

This quick and easy chili is mild and satisfyingly soupy. It's an easy meal using canned kidney beans and stewed tomatoes. We like it served with cornbread, but it can also be served over rice.

1. **BROWN THE BEEF.** Select Sauté and adjust the heat to High. Add the oil to the inner cooking pot. When it is hot, add the ground beef, onions, and garlic and cook, stirring occasionally, until the meat is browned, about 5 minutes.

2. **PREPARE THE SOUP.** Add the beans, tomato purée, stewed tomatoes, chili powder, and salt. Stir and heat to a slow boil.

3. **PRESSURE COOK.** Lock the lid into place and turn the valve to "sealing." Select Manual or Pressure Cook and adjust the pressure to High. Set the time for 15 minutes. When cooking ends, carefully turn the valve to "venting" to quick release the pressure.

4. **MASH THE BEANS.** Unlock and remove the lid. Use a fork to press the beans against the side of the Instant Pot® to mash them and thicken the soup.

TEX-MEX CHILI

Prep time: 10 MINUTES   *Sauté:* 10 MINUTES ON HIGH; 3 MINUTES ON MEDIUM
Pressure cook: 15 MINUTES ON HIGH   *Release:* QUICK   *Total time:* 48 MINUTES

SERVES 6

DAIRY-FREE OPTION
GLUTEN-FREE

EQUIPMENT
Measuring cups and
spoons, chef's knife, can
opener, wooden spoon or
silicone spatula

1½ pounds lean
ground beef

2 tablespoons vegetable oil

3 garlic cloves, minced

2 onions, finely chopped

3 tablespoons chili powder

1 teaspoon ground cumin

½ teaspoon dried oregano

1 teaspoon fine sea salt

½ teaspoon ground
black pepper

⅛ teaspoon cayenne
pepper (optional)

1½ cups low-sodium
beef broth

1 (14-ounce) can
tomato purée

1 (15-ounce) can pinto
beans, rinsed and drained

2 tablespoons cornmeal

½ cup shredded Cheddar
cheese (optional)

This delicious Tex-Mex Chili can be made in just 40 minutes,
and is a great dish to make when you have friends over to
watch a game or just hang out. It's mild, but you can add more
cayenne or hot sauce to kick up the heat. Top with diced red
onion or scallions, sour cream, diced avocado or guacamole,
and tortilla chips.

1. BROWN THE BEEF. Select Sauté and adjust the heat to High.
Add the ground beef to the inner cooking pot and brown,
about 5 minutes. Drain off any fat.

2. PREPARE THE REMAINING INGREDIENTS. Add the vegetable oil to the pot, along with the garlic, onions, chili powder,
cumin, oregano, salt, pepper, and cayenne (if using). Sauté
for 5 minutes. Add the broth and tomato purée and stir to
combine, scraping up any browned bits from the bottom of
the pot.

3. PRESSURE COOK. Lock the lid into place and turn the valve
to "sealing." Select Manual or Pressure Cook and adjust the
pressure to High. Set the time for 15 minutes. When cooking
ends, carefully turn the valve to "venting" to quick release
the pressure.

4. FINISH THE CHILI. Unlock and remove the lid. Select Sauté
and adjust the heat to Medium. Add the pinto beans, bring
to a simmer, and cook until the beans are heated, about
3 minutes. Sprinkle the cornmeal over the beans and stir until
thickened. Spoon into bowls and garnish with grated cheese
(if using).

Ingredient tip:

This recipe works great using the Pinto Beans on
page 38 in place of canned beans.

Pasta Puttanesca (page 66)

CHAPTER 5

Meatless Meals

CHEDDAR AND BROCCOLI BAKED POTATOES

Prep time: 10 MINUTES   *Pressure cook:* 1 MINUTE ON LOW; 15 MINUTES ON HIGH
Release: NATURAL FOR 12 MINUTES   *Total time:* 48 MINUTES

SERVES 4

GLUTEN-FREE
VEGETARIAN OPTION

EQUIPMENT
Measuring cups and
spoons, chef's knife, can
opener, steamer basket,
tongs or pot holder, trivet,
small bowl

2 cups broccoli florets

2 cups water, for
steaming, divided

4 small russet potatoes
(8 to 10 ounces each)

¾ cup evaporated milk

1 tablespoon
unsalted butter

2 cups shredded sharp
Cheddar cheese

1 teaspoon cornstarch

3 or 4 bacon slices, cooked
and crumbled (optional)

¼ cup chopped fresh
chives (optional)

When I first read about topping baked potatoes with broccoli,
I admit I was skeptical. But it turns out to be a great match,
especially when you add cheese sauce. It makes a great
vegetarian dinner (non-vegetarians can add the optional
bacon) or a substantial lunch.

1. PRESSURE COOK THE BROCCOLI. Put the broccoli in a
steamer basket. Pour 1 cup of water into the inner cooking
pot and place the steamer basket in it. Lock the lid into place.
Select Pressure Cook or Manual and adjust the pressure to
Low. Set the time to 1 minute. When cooking ends, carefully
turn the valve to "venting" to quick release the pressure.
Unlock and remove the lid. Use tongs or a pot holder to
remove the steamer basket. Pour out the water.

2. PRESSURE COOK THE POTATOES. Add a fresh 1 cup of water to
the inner cooking pot and place a trivet in the bottom. Place
the potatoes on the trivet; it's okay if they touch. Lock the lid
into place and turn the valve to "sealing." Select Manual or
Pressure Cook and adjust the pressure to High. Set the time
for 15 minutes. When cooking ends, let the pressure release
naturally for 12 minutes, then turn the valve to "venting" to
quick release the remaining pressure. Unlock and remove the
lid. Check the potatoes by inserting the tip of a knife into one;
it should pierce it easily. If the potatoes aren't quite done, lock
the lid back into place and cook for another 2 to 3 minutes.
Remove the potatoes and set them aside to cool slightly.

3. MAKE THE SAUCE. Remove the trivet and pour out the water. Wipe the pot dry. Select Sauté and adjust the heat to High. Add the evaporated milk and butter and bring to a simmer. While the milk heats, toss the cheese with the cornstarch in a small bowl. Add the cheese, a handful at a time, stirring to melt the cheese before adding the next handful.

4. FINISH THE POTATOES. Add the broccoli to the cheese sauce to warm up. Make a slit in the top of each potato and open up the potatoes by pushing the ends in toward the middle. Spoon some of the broccoli and cheese sauce into each potato and top with the bacon and chives (if using).

Variation tip:

If you like your potatoes with a crisper skin, heat the oven to 400°F while the potatoes pressure cook. Brush them with oil after cooking and place on a rimmed baking sheet. Roast them for about 15 minutes, then let cool slightly before serving.

STUFFED ACORN SQUASH

Prep time: 15 MINUTES   *Pressure cook:* 14 MINUTES ON HIGH   *Release:* NATURAL FOR 5 MINUTES   *Total time:* 44 MINUTES

SERVES 4

DAIRY-FREE
VEGAN

EQUIPMENT
Measuring cups and spoons, chef's knife, steamer basket, mixing spoon

2 tablespoons olive oil, divided

2 small acorn squash, halved lengthwise and seeded, stems trimmed

½ cup water, for steaming

1½ cups vegetable broth

5 bread slices, toasted and cut into ½-inch cubes

1 teaspoon dried sage (optional)

1 teaspoon onion powder

¼ teaspoon fine sea salt

½ teaspoon ground black pepper

⅓ cup dried cranberries

⅓ cup chopped pecans (optional)

This recipe uses the bowl-like shape of the acorn squash for stuffing. The stuffing and cranberries complement the squash's sweet and nutty flavor. You can use leftovers from Holiday Stuffing (page 109) to save even more time.

1. **PREPARE THE SQUASH.** Rub 1 tablespoon of oil on the outside of the squash. Place the squash halves, cut-sides up, in a steamer basket; it's okay if they overlap. Pour the water into the inner cooking pot and place the steamer basket in the pot.

2. **PRESSURE COOK.** Lock the lid into place and turn the valve to "sealing." Select Manual or Pressure Cook and set on High. Set the time for 14 minutes. When cooking ends, let the pressure release naturally for 5 minutes, then turn the valve to "venting" to quick release the remaining pressure.

3. **STUFF THE SQUASH.** Unlock and remove the lid. Remove the squash from the pot. Pour out the water and rinse the inner cooking pot. Add the remaining 1 tablespoon oil to the pot, along with the broth. Select Sauté and let the broth come to a simmer. Add the bread, sage (if using), onion powder, salt, pepper, and cranberries and stir until the bread absorbs the liquid and the stuffing becomes cohesive. Scoop the stuffing into the "bowls" of the squash halves and sprinkle with the pecans (if using).

Ingredient tip:

When picking out an acorn squash, look for one that has a smooth, dull skin. Use your fingers to gently press the squash; you want a firm squash with no soft spots.

SOUTHWESTERN SWEET POTATOES

Prep time: 10 MINUTES   *Pressure cook:* 25 MINUTES ON HIGH   *Sauté:* 5 MINUTES ON MEDIUM
Release: NATURAL FOR 10 MINUTES   *Total time:* 1 HOUR

SERVES 4

GLUTEN-FREE
VEGETARIAN

EQUIPMENT
Measuring cups and spoons, chef's knife, tall trivet, tongs

8 ounces dried black beans

3 to 3½ cups vegetable broth or water

1 small onion, quartered

1 garlic clove, peeled and smashed

2 teaspoons chili powder

2 teaspoons fine sea salt

¼ teaspoon cayenne pepper (optional)

4 small sweet potatoes (about 8 ounces each), scrubbed

½ cup sour cream

2 to 3 scallions, chopped (optional)

Sweet potatoes and black beans are a popular combo for vegetarian tacos, and I've adapted that duo for this flavorful dish. In a pinch, you can skip cooking your own beans and just add a can or two of beans, along with the seasonings, while the sweet potatoes cook.

1. PRESSURE COOK THE BEANS. Rinse the beans and discard any that float. Combine the beans and 3 cups of broth in the inner cooking pot. Stir in the onion, garlic, chili powder, salt, and cayenne (if using). Lock the lid into place. Select Pressure Cook or Manual and adjust the pressure to High. Set the time for 15 minutes. When cooking ends, let the pressure release naturally for 10 minutes, then turn the valve to "venting" to release the remaining pressure. Unlock and remove the lid.

2. PRESSURE COOK THE SWEET POTATOES. There should be liquid just covering the beans. If they are very dry, add the remaining ½ cup of broth. Put a tall trivet in the pot and place the sweet potatoes on top of the trivet. (If you don't have a tall trivet, the beans and liquid will come up over the top, which is okay, but will result in wetter sweet potatoes.) Lock the lid into place. Select Pressure Cook or Manual and adjust the pressure to High. Set the time for 10 minutes. When cooking ends, let the pressure release naturally for 8 minutes, then turn the valve to "venting" to quick release the remaining pressure. Unlock and remove the lid.

3. FINISH THE DISH. Use tongs to transfer the sweet potatoes to a plate and let them cool for a few minutes. If the beans are too soupy, select Sauté and adjust the heat to Medium. Simmer until the sauce has thickened to the consistency you want, about 5 minutes.

4. ASSEMBLE THE POTATOES. To assemble, cut a slit in the top of each sweet potato and open up the potatoes by pushing the ends in toward the middle. Spoon some beans onto the potatoes and top with the sour cream and scallions (if using).

MUSHROOM RISOTTO

Prep time: 15 MINUTES   *Sauté:* 5 MINUTES   *Pressure cook:* 14 MINUTES ON HIGH
Release: QUICK   *Total time:* 44 MINUTES

SERVES 4

GLUTEN-FREE
VEGETARIAN

EQUIPMENT
Measuring cups and spoons, chef's knife, wooden spoon or silicone spatula

4 tablespoons (½ stick) unsalted butter, divided

1 small onion, diced

3 garlic cloves, minced

8 ounces cremini mushrooms, thinly sliced

½ teaspoon fine sea salt

¼ teaspoon ground black pepper

¼ teaspoon dried thyme (optional)

1 cup Italian short-grain rice, such as Arborio

2 cups vegetable broth

2 cups baby spinach (optional)

¼ cup freshly grated Parmesan cheese

The traditional method for cooking risotto requires constant supervision, but the Instant Pot® makes it easy and still produces the creamy texture that makes risotto so popular. Most risotto recipes specify Italian Arborio rice, but I've found that you can use just about any type of rice you like (see the tip). The key is that you must never rinse the rice prior to cooking. The excess starch on the rice grains is crucial for achieving the desired texture.

1. **SAUTÉ THE VEGETABLES.** Select Sauté and adjust the heat to Medium. Add 2 tablespoons of butter to Instant Pot®. Once melted, add the onion, garlic, and mushrooms. Cook, stirring, for about 5 minutes, until the onion is translucent. Add the salt, pepper, thyme (if using), rice, and broth. Stir to mix.

2. **PRESSURE COOK.** Lock the lid into place and turn the valve to "sealing." Select Manual or Pressure Cook and adjust the pressure to High. Set the time for 6 minutes. When cooking ends, carefully turn the valve to "venting" to quick release the pressure.

3. **FINISH THE RISOTTO.** Unlock and remove the lid. Add the remaining 2 tablespoons of butter and the spinach (if using). Stir for 2 minutes, until the spinach wilts. Stir in the cheese.

Ingredient tip:

Arborio rice is a firm, short-grain white rice from Italy commonly used to make risotto. Similar Italian rice varieties sometimes used include Carnaroli, Vialone Nano, and Baldo. These grains are higher in starch than long-grain white rice. The extra starch prevents the rice from absorbing as much liquid, resulting in an especially creamy texture when cooked. You'll find Arborio rice alongside other rice at most supermarkets.

MACARONI AND CHEESE

Prep time: 5 MINUTES   *Pressure cook:* 4 MINUTES ON HIGH   *Release:* QUICK
Total time: 19 MINUTES

SERVES 6

VEGETARIAN

EQUIPMENT
Measuring cups
and spoons

4¼ cups water, divided

1 pound elbow macaroni

1 tablespoon fine sea salt

1 (12-ounce) can
evaporated milk

3 tablespoons
unsalted butter

3 cups sharp Cheddar
cheese, shredded

Mac and cheese earns a spot on the list of beloved comfort foods, along with Mashed Potatoes (page 104), Meatloaf (page 96), and Spaghetti and Meatballs (page 89). Through foods like these, my mom seemed to instill in me the idea that food is love, and I suppose I've passed this on to my own children. They will call me from college just to ask how to make one of my recipes whenever they are missing home.

1. PREPARE THE MACARONI. Combine 4 cups of water, the macaroni, and salt in the inner cooking pot.

2. PRESSURE COOK. Lock the lid into place and turn the valve to "sealing." Select Manual or Pressure Cook and adjust the pressure to High. Set the time for 4 minutes. When cooking ends, carefully turn the valve to "venting" to quick release the pressure.

3. FINISH THE DISH. Unlock and remove the lid. Add the milk, butter, and remaining ¼ cup of water. Stir to coat the macaroni. In small batches, add the cheese, while constantly stirring, until melted.

Variation tip:

You can change this dish up by using different cheeses or a mixture of cheeses, or make it "loaded" by stirring in cooked bacon, chopped scallions, sour cream, and other flavorful add-ins. Or top it with a layer of toasted bread crumbs for added texture.

PASTA PUTTANESCA

Prep time: 5 MINUTES   *Pressure cook:* 5 MINUTES ON HIGH   *Release:* QUICK
Total time: 20 MINUTES

SERVES 6

DAIRY-FREE
VEGAN

EQUIPMENT
Measuring cups and
spoons, mixing spoon

3 garlic cloves, minced

1 (32-ounce) jar pasta sauce

3 cups water

4 cups dried pasta, such as
penne or rigatoni

¼ teaspoon crushed
red pepper flakes

1 tablespoon capers

½ cup pitted Kalamata
olives, sliced

1 teaspoon fine sea salt

¼ teaspoon ground
black pepper

2 teaspoons grated
lemon zest

I started making this flavorful Neapolitan dish because of
Lemony Snicket. One of my kids requested it after reading
that the Baudelaire children prepared it in one of the books
in *A Series of Unfortunate Events*. It couldn't be simpler in
the Instant Pot®— just add the ingredients and come back
to a pasta dinner! This recipe is vegan but see the tip for
how to add in anchovies, which are traditional. Garnish with
shredded cheese or chopped fresh basil, if you like.

1. **ASSEMBLE THE INGREDIENTS.** Combine all of the ingredients in the inner cooking pot and stir to coat the pasta.

2. **PRESSURE COOK.** Lock the lid into place and turn the valve
to "sealing." Select Manual or Pressure Cook and adjust the
pressure to High. Set the time for 5 minutes. When cooking
ends, carefully turn the valve to "venting" to quick release the
pressure. Unlock and remove the lid.

Variation tip:

If you eat fish, go ahead and add anchovies for additional flavor. Use 1 (2-ounce) can of anchovies packed
in oil (drained), adding it to the pot along with the other
ingredients. I think their salty, pungent flavor offsets the
sweetness of a typical tomato-based sauce.

PEANUT NOODLES

Prep time: 5 MINUTES   *Pressure cook:* 0 MINUTES ON LOW   *Sauté:* 3 MINUTES ON LOW
Release: QUICK   *Total time:* 18 MINUTES

SERVES 4

DAIRY-FREE
VEGAN

EQUIPMENT
Measuring cups
and spoons

2½ cups water or
vegetable broth

2 tablespoons soy sauce

3 tablespoons toasted
sesame oil, divided

½ teaspoon
granulated garlic

2 packages ramen noodles,
seasoning packets
discarded

⅓ cup peanut butter

1 cup frozen "stir-fry"
vegetables, thawed

Inexpensive and quick-cooking, ramen noodles are a college student's dream. But they can get pretty boring pretty fast. This easy recipe upgrades them to a delicious Asian-inspired dinner—and it even has vegetables! Choose smooth or crunchy peanut butter, whichever you prefer.

1. PREPARE THE NOODLES. Combine the water, soy sauce, 1 tablespoon of sesame oil, and the granulated garlic in the inner cooking pot. Add the noodles, breaking up each block into 3 or 4 pieces and arranging them in the pot in a single layer as much as possible.

2. PRESSURE COOK. Lock the lid into place and turn the valve to "sealing." Select Pressure Cook or Manual and adjust the pressure to Low. Set the time for 0 minutes. When cooking ends, carefully turn the valve to "venting" to quick release the pressure.

3. FINISH THE NOODLES. Unlock and remove the lid. Select Sauté and adjust the heat to Low. Add the remaining 2 tablespoons of sesame oil and the peanut butter and stir gently until the sauce is smooth and the noodles are separated. Add the vegetables and stir into the noodles to warm through, about 2 minutes.

Sesame Chicken (page 78)

Poultry

CHICKEN CAESAR SALAD

Prep time: 13 MINUTES   *Pressure cook:* POULTRY SETTING FOR 5 MINUTES   *Release:* QUICK
Total time: 28 MINUTES

SERVES 2

GLUTEN-FREE OPTION

EQUIPMENT
Measuring cups and spoons, chef's knife, large bowl, small bowl

FOR THE CHICKEN

2 boneless, skinless chicken breasts

½ teaspoon fine sea salt

¼ teaspoon ground black pepper

1 garlic clove, minced (optional)

⅔ cup water or chicken broth

FOR THE SALAD

1 romaine lettuce heart

¼ cup croutons (optional)

½ cup grated Parmesan cheese, divided

1 garlic clove, minced

¼ teaspoon grated lemon zest

2 tablespoons freshly squeezed lemon juice

2 tablespoons mayonnaise

3 tablespoons olive oil

½ teaspoon fine sea salt

This recipe is super easy. You prep and cook the chicken breasts first, which is a great method to have under your belt so you can always have cooked chicken breast on hand. While the chicken cooks, you can prepare the salad and the dressing.

1. **PREPARE THE CHICKEN.** Season the chicken breasts with the salt and pepper. Put them in the inner cooking pot, along with the garlic (if using) and water.

2. **PRESSURE COOK.** Lock the lid into place and turn the valve to "sealing." Select the Poultry setting and adjust the time to 5 minutes.

3. **PREPARE THE SALAD WHILE THE CHICKEN COOKS.** Tear the lettuce leaves into bite-size pieces and place them in a large bowl. Add the croutons (if using) and ¼ cup of cheese. Toss gently.

4. **MAKE THE DRESSING.** In a small bowl, combine the garlic, lemon zest and juice, and remaining ¼ cup of cheese. Whisk in the mayonnaise. Gradually whisk in the oil. Season with the salt.

5. **REMOVE THE CHICKEN.** When cooking ends, carefully turn the valve to "venting" to quick release the pressure. Unlock and remove the lid.

6. FINISH THE SALAD. Cut the chicken into strips. Divide the lettuce mixture between two serving bowls. Top each with half of the chicken strips and drizzle with the dressing.

Variation tip:

This dressing is thin. If you like your dressing thicker, add more mayonnaise and Parmesan cheese.

Recipe tip:

When you've got cooked chicken in your refrigerator, you have a great grab-and-go protein option to help fuel your body and brain. Follow steps 1, 2, and 5 for cooking chicken breasts (you can even double it), then shred or dice the meat to top salads or pasta, mix it into soups, or use as a taco or burrito filling.

CHICKEN AND BROCCOLI CHEESY RICE

Prep time: 5 MINUTES   *Pressure cook:* 10 MINUTES ON HIGH   *Release:* QUICK
Total time: 25 MINUTES

SERVES 4

GLUTEN-FREE

EQUIPMENT
Measuring cups
and spoons

Nonstick cooking spray

4 cups low-sodium
chicken broth

1 cup long-grain white rice

½ teaspoon fine sea salt

¼ teaspoon ground
black pepper

2 boneless, skinless
chicken breasts, cut into
1-inch pieces

4 cups broccoli florets

1½ cups shredded
Cheddar cheese

This one-pot dish is so easy and so satisfying, with bites of chicken breast, a splash of color from the broccoli, and perfect rice all smothered in cheese. When it appears on our weekly menu, any of my children heading out the door will say, "Save me a bowl for dinner, please?"

1. **PREPARE TO COOK.** Spray the inner cooking pot with non-stick cooking spray. Add the broth, rice, salt, pepper, chicken, and broccoli.

2. **PRESSURE COOK.** Lock the lid into place and turn the valve to "sealing." Select Manual or Pressure Cook and adjust the pressure to High. Set the time for 10 minutes. When cooking ends, carefully turn the valve to "venting" to quick release the pressure.

3. **FINISH THE DISH.** Unlock and remove the lid. Stir in the cheese until melted.

Variation tip:

You can use different proteins to vary this dish. Try substituting kielbasa or another smoked sausage for the chicken.

ARROZ CON POLLO

Prep time: 10 MINUTES *Sauté:* 6 MINUTES ON MEDIUM *Pressure cook:* 10 MINUTES ON HIGH
Release: NATURAL FOR 10 MINUTES *Total time:* 46 MINUTES

SERVES 4

DAIRY-FREE
GLUTEN-FREE

EQUIPMENT
Measuring cups and
spoons, chef's knife,
wooden spoon or
silicone spatula

4 tablespoons olive
oil, divided

3 boneless, skinless
chicken breasts, cut into
small pieces

2 teaspoons fine sea salt

¼ teaspoon ground
black pepper

1 cup finely chopped onion

1 cup chopped
green pepper

1 cup chopped bell
red pepper

3 garlic cloves, minced

2 cups long-grain
white rice

2 teaspoons ground cumin

3 cups low-sodium
chicken broth

1 (14-ounce) can
fire-roasted tomatoes

2 cups frozen peas
and carrots

½ cup green olives, plus
1 tablespoon of their brine
(optional)

This flavorful Spanish-style dish of rice (*arroz*) and chicken
(*pollo*) is the ultimate comfort food. In my house, we call it
"ACP" for short—that shows how often we make it! It requires
minimal effort and is a complete meal; add Black Beans
(page 37) if you like.

1. BROWN THE CHICKEN. Select Sauté and adjust the heat to
Medium. Add 2 tablespoons of the oil to the inner cooking
pot. When the oil is hot, season the chicken with the salt and
pepper and add it to the pot. Cook for 3 minutes on each side,
or until golden brown. Transfer the chicken to a plate.

2. SAUTÉ THE VEGETABLES AND RICE. Add the remaining
2 tablespoons of oil to the pot, and then add the onion,
green and red peppers, and garlic. Cook the vegetables for
3 minutes. Add the rice and stir to coat the grains. Add the
cumin, broth, tomatoes with their juices, frozen peas and
carrots, and olives and brine (if using). Return the chicken to
the pot.

3. PRESSURE COOK. Lock the lid into place and turn the valve
to "sealing." Select Manual or Pressure Cook and adjust the
pressure to High. Set the time for 10 minutes. When cooking
ends, let the pressure release naturally for 10 minutes, then
turn the valve to "venting" to quick release the remaining
pressure.

4. FLUFF THE RICE. Unlock and remove the lid. Fluff the rice
with a fork before serving.

SMOTHERED CHICKEN WITH MUSHROOMS

Prep time: 15 MINUTES   *Sauté:* 12 MINUTES ON MEDIUM   *Pressure cook:* 20 MINUTES ON HIGH
Release: NATURAL FOR 5 MINUTES   *Total time:* 1 HOUR 2 MINUTES

SERVES 4

EQUIPMENT
Measuring cups and
spoons, chef's knife,
can opener, shallow
bowl, wooden spoon or
silicone spatula

¼ cup all-purpose flour

4 bone-in, skinless chicken
thighs or breasts

1 teaspoon fine sea salt

1 teaspoon ground
black pepper

4 tablespoons olive oil,
divided

2 bacon slices, cut into
1-inch pieces (optional)

8 ounces
mushrooms, sliced

1 small onion, chopped

2 garlic cloves, minced

1 cup low-sodium
chicken broth

1 cup tomato sauce

1 (10-ounce) can
condensed cream of
mushroom soup

When I first got married, my mom gave me a Craig Claiborne
cookbook. I wanted to cook (or at the very least eat) everything in it, especially his recipe for a slow-cooked whole
chicken smothered in a rich gravy. Oh, it was divine. For me,
this recipe reproduces that amazing flavor, but with far less
time and effort. I like to serve it over rice or noodles.

1. **PREPARE THE CHICKEN.** Put the flour in a wide, shallow
bowl. Season the chicken with the salt and pepper. Use
2 tablespoons of oil to coat each piece of chicken, then
roll it in the flour to coat.

2. **BROWN THE CHICKEN AND VEGETABLES.** Select Sauté and
adjust the heat to Medium. Add the remaining 2 tablespoons
of oil to the pot. When the oil is hot, add the chicken and
cook until browned, about 3 minutes on each side. Add the
bacon (if using), mushrooms, onion, and garlic and sauté for
5 minutes. Add the broth and stir to loosen any ingredients
that may have stuck to the bottom of the pot. Add the tomato
sauce and cook, stirring, for 1 minute.

3. **PRESSURE COOK.** Lock the lid into place and turn the valve
to "sealing." Select Manual or Pressure Cook and adjust the
pressure to High. Set the time for 20 minutes. When cooking
ends, let the pressure release naturally for 5 minutes, then
turn the valve to "venting" to quick release the remaining
pressure.

4. **FINISH THE SAUCE.** Unlock and remove the lid and stir in the
cream of mushroom soup until heated through.

CHICKEN CHILE VERDE

Prep time: 5 MINUTES   *Pressure cook:* 15 MINUTES ON HIGH   *Release:* QUICK
Total time: 30 MINUTES

SERVES 4

DAIRY-FREE
GLUTEN-FREE

EQUIPMENT
Measuring cups and
spoons, chef's knife,
can opener, mixing
spoon, tongs

3 pounds bone-in, skin-on
chicken drumsticks
and/or thighs

1 (15-ounce) jar salsa verde
(green chile salsa)

1 (27-ounce) can roasted
poblano peppers, drained

1 (7-ounce) jar chopped
green chiles, drained

1 tablespoon chopped
jalapeño (optional)

1 onion, chopped

4 teaspoons minced garlic

1 tablespoon ground cumin

1 teaspoon fine sea salt

This green chile chicken is not your standard chicken
dish. The tender dark meat is smothered in a rich sauce
of green (verde) chile salsa and roasted poblano peppers
for an irresistible flavor. It's a one-pot meal that is ready in
30 minutes. Serve it as a soup or over rice or noodles.

1. COMBINE THE INGREDIENTS. Combine the chicken, salsa
verde, poblano peppers, green chiles, jalapeño (if using),
onion, garlic, cumin, and salt in the inner cooking pot. Stir to
mix well.

2. PRESSURE COOK. Lock the lid into place and turn the valve
to "sealing." Select Manual or Pressure Cook and adjust the
pressure to High. Set the time for 15 minutes. When cooking
ends, carefully turn the valve to "venting" to quick release
the pressure.

3. SHRED THE CHICKEN. Unlock and remove the lid. Use tongs
to transfer the chicken to a plate. When the chicken is cool
enough to handle, remove and discard the bones and skin.
Shred the chicken with two forks or cut it into bite-size pieces.
Return the chicken to the sauce and stir.

Ingredient tip:

Salsa verde is a green salsa made with tomatillos, which
look similar to green tomatoes, but are tarter. (They are
more closely related to gooseberries than to tomatoes.)
Their flavor is a nice balance for the heat in the chiles.

SIMPLE TUSCAN CHICKEN

Prep time: 10 MINUTES   *Sauté:* 10 MINUTES ON MEDIUM, DIVIDED
Pressure cook: 3 MINUTES ON HIGH   *Release:* QUICK   *Total time:* 33 MINUTES

SERVES 4

GLUTEN-FREE

EQUIPMENT
Measuring cups and spoons, chef's knife, plastic wrap, pan or rolling pin, tongs

2 pounds boneless, skinless chicken breasts

1 tablespoon Italian seasoning

½ teaspoon fine sea salt

4 garlic cloves, minced

2 tablespoons olive oil

¾ cup low-sodium chicken broth

¾ cup heavy cream

¾ cup grated Parmesan cheese

½ cup oil-packed sun-dried tomatoes, drained

2 cups chopped fresh spinach

For college kids, limited budgets can be a challenge, meaning dining out doesn't happen often. When one of my kids was planning a date night, they knew a popular pasta restaurant was their date's favorite. The budget was tight, so we created this recipe to offer all of the flavors of the restaurant's version at a fraction of the cost. The date went well, with cooking together being part of the experience. It might go down in history as one of the best college dates ever! Serve the chicken and sauce over pasta.

1. PREPARE THE CHICKEN. Cut the chicken breasts in half lengthwise. One at a time, place the chicken breasts between two pieces of plastic wrap. On top of a protected surface, like a cutting board on the counter, use a pan or rolling pin to pound the meat to about ½ inch thick. Season the chicken with the Italian seasoning, salt, and garlic, pressing the seasonings into the chicken with your fingertips.

2. BROWN THE CHICKEN. Add the oil to the inner cooking pot, select Sauté, and adjust the heat to Medium. When the oil is hot, add the chicken and brown for 2 minutes on each side. Remove the chicken and add the broth, stirring to loosen any chicken pieces that may have stuck to the bottom. Return the chicken to the pot.

3. PRESSURE COOK. Lock the lid into place and turn the valve to "sealing." Select Manual or Pressure Cook and adjust the pressure to High. Set the time for 3 minutes. When cooking ends, carefully turn the valve to "venting" to quick release the pressure.

4. PREPARE THE SAUCE. Unlock and remove the lid. Use tongs to transfer the chicken pieces to a plate. Select Sauté on the Instant Pot® and adjust the heat to Medium. Whisk the cream into the broth, stirring to combine. Bring to a simmer and cook, stirring occasionally, for 5 minutes. Add the cheese and sun-dried tomatoes and stir until the cheese melts. Add the spinach and stir just until the spinach wilts.

CHICKEN LO MEIN

Prep time: 10 MINUTES   *Sauté:* 5 MINUTES ON MEDIUM   *Pressure cook:* 5 MINUTES ON HIGH
Release: QUICK   *Total time:* 30 MINUTES

SERVES 4

DAIRY-FREE

EQUIPMENT
Measuring cups and spoons, chef's knife, wooden spoon or silicone spatula, medium bowl

1 tablespoon toasted sesame oil

1½ pounds boneless, skinless chicken breast, cut into bite-size pieces

1 garlic clove, minced

8 ounces dried linguine, broken in half

1 cup snow peas

1 cup broccoli florets

1 carrot, peeled and thinly sliced

1½ cups low-sodium chicken broth

1 tablespoon soy sauce

1 tablespoon fish sauce (see tip)

1 tablespoon Shaoxing rice wine (see tip)

1 teaspoon grated fresh ginger

1 tablespoon brown sugar

My husband grew eating at Sam Wo in San Francisco's Chinatown and loved their lo mein; he would happily eat it any day of the week. This recipe comes close. My husband devours it, as do my kids, who love noisily slurping the noodles.

1. PREPARE THE CHICKEN, VEGETABLES, AND NOODLES. Select Sauté and adjust the heat to Medium. Add the sesame oil. When the oil is hot, add the chicken and garlic and cook until the garlic is light brown and chicken is opaque, about 5 minutes. Fan the noodles across the bottom of the pot. Add the snow peas, broccoli, and carrot on top of the noodles.

2. MAKE THE SAUCE. In a medium bowl, combine the broth, soy sauce, fish sauce, rice wine, ginger, and brown sugar. Stir until the sugar is dissolved. Pour the sauce over the vegetables in the pot.

3. PRESSURE COOK. Lock the lid into place and turn the valve to "sealing." Select Manual and adjust the pressure to High. Set the time for 5 minutes. When cooking ends, carefully turn the valve to "venting" to quick release the pressure.

4. FINISH THE DISH. Unlock and remove the lid. Stir the noodles, breaking up any clumps, until the liquid is absorbed.

Ingredient tip:

If you don't have fish sauce, you can substitute an equal amount of soy sauce. You can also substitute an equal amount of apple juice for the Shaoxing rice wine.

THAI CHICKEN RICE BOWLS

Prep time: 7 MINUTES   *Sauté:* 6 MINUTES ON MEDIUM   *Pressure cook:* 10 MINUTES ON HIGH
Release: NATURAL FOR 10 MINUTES   *Total time:* 33 MINUTES

SERVES 4

DAIRY-FREE

EQUIPMENT
Measuring cups and spoons, wooden spoon or silicone spatula, medium bowl, whisk

2 tablespoons toasted sesame oil

2 pounds boneless, skinless chicken breast

½ cup Thai sweet chili sauce (see tip)

3 tablespoons soy sauce

1½ teaspoons fish sauce (see tip)

1½ teaspoons minced fresh ginger

1 garlic clove, minced

1 teaspoon freshly squeezed lime juice

1 teaspoon hot sauce

1 tablespoon peanut butter (optional)

1 cup long-grain white rice

2 cups low-sodium chicken broth

Thai food appeals to those who like a hit of spice in their food, especially when it is balanced with salty, sour, sweet, and bitter flavors. This is truly a one-pot meal from start to finish, and it is loaded with flavor. It is one of my favorite dishes to make in the Instant Pot®.

1. BROWN THE CHICKEN. Select Sauté and adjust the heat to Medium. Add the oil to the inner cooking pot. When the oil is hot, add the chicken and brown, about 3 minutes per side. Transfer the chicken to a plate.

2. MAKE THE SAUCE. In a medium bowl, whisk the sweet chili sauce, soy sauce, fish sauce, ginger, garlic, lime juice, hot sauce, and peanut butter (if using) until well combined.

3. ASSEMBLE THE DISH. Add the rice to the pot. Place the chicken breasts on top of the rice. Pour the sauce over the chicken and rice. Pour in the broth.

4. PRESSURE COOK. Lock the lid into place and turn the valve to "sealing." Select Manual and adjust the pressure to High. Set the time for 10 minutes. When cooking ends, let the pressure release naturally.

5. FINISH THE DISH. Unlock and remove the lid. Transfer the chicken to a clean plate. Using a hand mixer (see page 93) or two forks, shred the chicken. Stir the rice, divide it between four serving bowls, and top with the chicken.

Ingredient tip:

Thai sweet chile sauce is more sweet than spicy, with flecks of red chili and garlic. It's typically served as a dipping sauce for spring rolls. You can find it in the international foods aisle in most supermarkets. If you don't have fish sauce, you can substitute an equal amount of soy sauce.

CHICKEN EGG ROLL WRAPS

Prep time: 10 MINUTES   *Pressure cook:* 2 MINUTES ON HIGH   *Release:* QUICK
Sauté: 2 MINUTES ON HIGH   *Total time:* 24 MINUTES

SERVES 4

DAIRY-FREE

EQUIPMENT
Measuring cups and spoons, chef's knife, tongs, slotted spoon

3 tablespoons soy sauce

1 tablespoon rice vinegar, white wine vinegar, or lime juice

1 teaspoon granulated sugar

4 cups shredded cabbage or coleslaw mix

1 large carrot, shredded (about ½ cup)

½ cup chopped mushrooms

3 scallions, chopped

2 teaspoons minced garlic (see tip)

1 teaspoon grated fresh ginger (see tip)

1 tablespoon toasted sesame oil

12 ounces chicken tenders or chicken breast, cut into 1-inch strips

4 to 6 flour tortillas or other wraps, warmed

You can make these delicious, healthy egg roll wraps in less time than it takes to order takeout. The filling is great over leftover rice or mixed with cooked ramen noodles. Don't worry if you don't have all the vegetables; all you really need is the cabbage.

1. PREPARE THE INGREDIENTS. Combine the soy sauce, vinegar, and sugar in the inner cooking pot. Add the cabbage, carrot, mushrooms, scallions, garlic, ginger, and sesame oil and stir. Lay the chicken tenders on top.

2. PRESSURE COOK THE FILLING. Lock the lid into place and turn the valve to "sealing." Select Pressure Cook or Manual and adjust the pressure to High. Set the time for 2 minutes. When cooking ends, carefully turn the valve to "venting" to quick release the pressure.

3. FINISH THE FILLING. Unlock and remove the lid. Use tongs to transfer the chicken to a plate. When the chicken is cool enough to handle, shred it with two forks or cut it into bite-size pieces. (Don't worry if the center of the chicken is not quite done; it will cook further.) Stir the chicken back into the vegetables. Select Sauté and adjust the heat to High. Bring the mixture to a boil for a minute or so, just to reduce the liquid by about half and finish cooking the chicken if necessary.

4. ASSEMBLE. Using a slotted spoon, scoop out the filling onto the wraps, leaving most of the liquid behind so the wraps don't get soggy. Fold the wraps around the filling, tucking in the edges.

Ingredient tip:

You can also buy jars or tubes of minced garlic and ginger, or frozen cubes of both, in most grocery stores. In a pinch, you can substitute ¼ teaspoon ground ginger and ½ teaspoon garlic powder.

TERIYAKI CHICKEN

Prep time: 15 MINUTES   *Sauté:* 4 MINUTES ON HIGH   *Broil:* 5 MINUTES
Pressure cook: 8 MINUTES ON HIGH   *Release:* NATURAL FOR 5 MINUTES   *Total time:* 47 MINUTES

SERVES 4

DAIRY-FREE

EQUIPMENT
Measuring cups and spoons, chef's knife, rimmed baking sheet with rack

4 to 6 bone-in, skin-on chicken thighs

½ teaspoon kosher salt

2 tablespoons olive oil

¼ cup low-sodium chicken broth

¼ cup plus 2 tablespoons teriyaki sauce, divided (see tip to make your own)

1 large red bell pepper, seeded and cut into 1-inch chunks

1 (8-ounce) can unsweetened pineapple chunks, drained

If you think you prefer chicken breasts to thighs, I hope this recipe will have you rethinking that. Chicken thighs are cheaper than breasts, more forgiving if overcooked, and tastier, too! Sweet and savory teriyaki sauce is a good introduction to the wonders of chicken thighs, and I'll bet this recipe will be the one to change your mind.

1. **SEAR THE CHICKEN.** Season the chicken thighs on both sides with the salt. Select Sauté and adjust to More for high heat. Add the oil to the pot and heat until it shimmers and flows like water. Add the chicken thighs, skin-side down, and let them cook, undisturbed, for about 4 minutes, until the skin is golden brown. Transfer the thighs to a plate.

2. **MAKE THE SAUCE.** Pour out the fat. Add the broth and scrape the bottom of the pan to release the browned bits. Add 2 tablespoons of teriyaki sauce and stir to combine. Add the bell pepper chunks and chicken thighs, skin-side up.

3. **PRESSURE COOK THE CHICKEN.** Lock the lid into place and turn the valve to "sealing." Select Manual and adjust the pressure to High. Set the time to 8 minutes. When cooking ends, let the pressure release naturally for 5 minutes, then turn the valve to "venting" to quick release the remaining pressure.

4. **CRISP THE CHICKEN.** While the pressure releases on the chicken, preheat the oven to broil. Remove the chicken thighs from the pan and place them on a rack set over a rimmed baking sheet. Brush with the remaining ¼ cup of teriyaki sauce. Broil the chicken thighs for 3 to 5 minutes, until browned.

5. FINISH THE DISH. While the chicken broils, add the pine-apple chunks to the pot. Select Sauté and adjust the heat to Medium. Bring to a simmer to thicken the sauce and warm the pineapple through. When the chicken is done, top it with the peppers and pineapple, and drizzle with the sauce.

Recipe tip:

To make your own teriyaki sauce, just whisk together ½ cup soy sauce, 3 tablespoons honey, 1 tablespoon rice vinegar, 2 teaspoons minced fresh ginger, and 2 minced garlic cloves.

THANKSGIVING TURKEY AND GRAVY

Prep time: 25 MINUTES, PLUS 10 MINUTES TO REST   *Pressure cook:* 15 MINUTES ON HIGH
Release: NATURAL FOR 8 MINUTES   *Roast:* 15 MINUTES   *Sauté:* 5 MINUTES ON MEDIUM
Total time: 1 HOUR 28 MINUTES

SERVES 4

EQUIPMENT
Measuring cups and
spoons, trivet, rimmed
baking sheet with rack,
small bowl

1 (4½- to 5-pound) bone-in
turkey breast

4 teaspoons poultry
seasoning

¾ teaspoon fine sea salt

1 cup low-sodium
chicken broth

2 tablespoons unsalted
butter, melted

2 tablespoons
all-purpose flour

2 tablespoons heavy cream
(optional)

If you can't go home for Thanksgiving, you can still prepare
a delicious dinner for your friends, starting with a perfectly
cooked turkey breast and irresistible gravy. Get your friends to
make a few side dishes, and finish the feast with Pumpkin Pie
(page 120). Who knows? Maybe a new tradition will be born.

1. PREPARE THE TURKEY. Pat the turkey breast dry. Mix
together the poultry seasoning and salt. Rub about half of the
mixture on the skin and in the cavity on the underside of the
breast; reserve the rest.

2. PRESSURE COOK. Pour the chicken broth into the inner
cooking pot. Place a trivet in the pot. Place the turkey breast,
skin-side up if possible, on the trivet. Lock the lid into place
and turn the valve to "sealing." Select Pressure Cook or
Manual and adjust the pressure to High. Set the time to
15 minutes. When cooking ends, let the pressure release naturally for 8 minutes, then turn the valve to "venting" to quick
release the remaining pressure. Unlock and remove the lid.

3. ROAST THE TURKEY. While the turkey pressure cooks, preheat the oven to 400°F. Mix the remaining seasoning mixture
with the butter. When the turkey is ready, remove it from the
pot and place it, skin-side up, on a rack set over a rimmed
baking sheet. Brush the turkey skin with the seasoned butter.
Roast the turkey for 10 to 15 minutes, until the skin is browned
and the interior temperature reaches at least 155°F.

4. MAKE THE GRAVY. While the turkey roasts, remove the trivet from the inner cooking pot. Remove about ½ cup of the cooking liquid and leave the rest in the pot. Select Sauté and adjust the heat to Medium. In a small bowl, stir together the flour and the ½ cup cooking liquid. When the liquid in the pot is simmering, gradually stir in the flour mixture. Cook for 3 to 5 minutes, until the gravy comes to a boil and is thickened. For a creamier gravy, stir in the optional cream.

5. FINISH THE TURKEY. When the turkey is done, remove it from the oven and let it rest for about 10 minutes before slicing.

Pork Fried Rice (page 88)

Pork and Beef

PORK FRIED RICE

Prep time: 10 MINUTES, PLUS 5 MINUTES TO REST   *Sauté:* 7 MINUTES ON MEDIUM
Pressure cook: RICE SETTING (ABOUT 14 MINUTES)   *Release:* NATURAL FOR 10 MINUTES
Total time: 51 MINUTES

SERVES 8

DAIRY-FREE

EQUIPMENT
Measuring cups and spoons, chef's knife, small bowl

3 tablespoons vegetable oil, divided

1 small onion, finely chopped

2 (6-ounce) pork chops, cut into ½-inch pieces

1 teaspoon fine sea salt

½ teaspoon ground black pepper

3 cups water

2 cups long-grain rice

1 large egg, beaten

3 tablespoons soy sauce

½ cup frozen peas and carrots

2 scallions, finely chopped (optional)

We live in a town without good Chinese food, and yet it's something we crave often. This fried rice recipe is incredibly easy and satisfies the cravings. It's also extremely budget friendly, so even if you have good takeout options, save some dough and make this fried rice in your Instant Pot® instead.

1. SAUTÉ THE VEGETABLES AND PORK. Select Sauté and adjust the heat to Medium. Add 1 tablespoon of oil to the inner cooking pot. When it's hot, add the onion and cook, stirring occasionally, for 2 minutes. Season the pork with the salt and pepper. Add the pork to the pot and cook, stirring occasionally, for about 5 minutes. Transfer the pork and onion to a small bowl.

2. PRESSURE COOK THE RICE. Add the water to the pot and scrape the bottom of the pan to remove any browned pieces. Add the rice. Lock the lid into place and turn the valve to "sealing." Select Rice, which will automatically set the cooking time based on the amount of rice and water in the pot. When cooking ends, let the pressure release naturally for 10 minutes, then turn the valve to "venting" to quick release the remaining pressure.

3. FINISH THE RICE. Unlock and remove the lid. Stir the rice and create a well in the center so you can see the bottom of the pot. Add the remaining 2 tablespoons of oil into the center. Pour the beaten egg into the hole and stir quickly. Stir in the soy sauce and the pork and onions. Add the peas and carrots to the rice and allow to rest for 5 minutes to heat through. Garnish with the scallions (if using).

SPAGHETTI AND MEATBALLS

Prep time: 5 MINUTES   *Pressure cook:* 10 MINUTES ON HIGH   *Release:* QUICK
Total time: 25 MINUTES

SERVES 6

EQUIPMENT
Measuring cups
and spoons

1 pound frozen meatballs

1 pound dried spaghetti

2 tablespoons olive oil

1 (24-ounce) jar
pasta sauce

3 cups water

1 cup shredded Cheddar
or mozzarella cheese

Fresh basil, for garnish
(optional)

Spaghetti and meatballs is a dinner just about everyone can agree on. This Instant Pot® recipe makes over the classic so it's simpler than ever. It requires just a few ingredients (you probably already have most of them) and can be on the table in less than 30 minutes! This quick one-pot meal has the taste and texture of a baked spaghetti more than a stove-top sauce. Try adding fresh spinach leaves to the top of the pot for cooking or swap the marinara for Alfredo. When I have leftover Meatloaf (page 96), I substitute it for the meatballs.

1. **PREPARE THE INGREDIENTS.** Arrange the frozen meatballs in the bottom of the Instant Pot®. Place the uncooked spaghetti on top of the meat, fanning the noodles out. Drizzle the oil over the pasta and then pour the sauce on top. Add the water to the pot.

2. **PRESSURE COOK.** Lock the lid into place and turn the valve to "sealing." Select Manual or Pressure Cook and adjust the pressure to High. Set the time for 10 minutes. When cooking ends, carefully turn the valve to "venting" to quick release the pressure.

3. **FINISH THE SPAGHETTI.** Unlock and remove the lid. Stir in the cheese and garnish with the basil (if using).

Variation tip:

You can use Italian sausage in place of the meatballs. Select Sauté on the Instant Pot® and add 1 tablespoon of olive oil. Add 1 pound of loose Italian sausage and cook, stirring frequently, until browned, about 5 minutes. Transfer the sausage to a bowl and wipe out any excess fat from the pot using a paper towel. Return the sausage to the pot and continue with the recipe.

TACO MEAT FROM FROZEN

Prep time: 5 MINUTES   *Pressure cook:* 25 MINUTES ON HIGH   *Release:* QUICK
Sauté: 5 MINUTES ON MEDIUM   *Total time:* 45 MINUTES

SERVES 4

DAIRY-FREE
GLUTEN-FREE

EQUIPMENT
Measuring cup, mixing
spoon, trivet

1 cup water or low-sodium
beef broth

1 packet taco seasoning mix
(see tip)

1 pound frozen ground beef

You meant to defrost the ground beef before you left for class,
but come home to find you forgot. Don't worry, dinner doesn't
have to be takeout. With the Instant Pot®, you can make
delicious taco filling using frozen ground beef. Add a package
of tortillas or taco shells, shredded cheese, and salsa, and
you've got a satisfying dinner with very little effort.

1. **PREPARE THE INGREDIENTS.** Combine the water and taco
seasoning in the inner cooking pot and stir to mix well. Place a
trivet in the pot and place the frozen meat on top.

2. **PRESSURE COOK.** Lock the lid and turn the valve to "sealing."
Select Manual or Pressure Cook and adjust the pressure to
High. Set the time for 25 minutes. When cooking ends, care-
fully turn the valve to "venting" to quick release the pressure.

3. **FINISH THE MEAT.** Unlock and remove the lid. Remove the
meat and trivet. Return the meat to the inner cooking pot.
Select Sauté and adjust the heat to Medium. Begin breaking
up the meat with a spoon. Allow to simmer and reduce, stirring occasionally, until the meat is to the desired consistency,
about 5 minutes.

Ingredient tip:

Check the taco seasoning mix label to ensure it's
dairy-free or gluten-free. You can also make your
own taco seasoning, which will save money and let
you control exactly what goes in it. In a small bowl,
combine 6 tablespoons chili powder, ¼ cup paprika,
3 tablespoons onion powder, 2 tablespoons ground
cumin, and 1 tablespoon garlic powder. Stir to mix well.
Use 5 tablespoons of this mixture per pound of meat
or as a substitute for 1 envelope of store-bought taco
seasoning mix.

SLOPPY JOES

Prep time: 10 MINUTES   *Sauté:* 7 MINUTES ON MEDIUM   *Pressure cook:* 12 MINUTES ON HIGH
Release: QUICK   *Total time:* 39 MINUTES

SERVES 4

DAIRY-FREE

EQUIPMENT
Measuring cups and spoons, chef's knife, mixing spoon, paper towels

1 pound ground beef, divided

½ cup chopped onion

½ cup chopped green bell pepper

¼ cup water or low-sodium beef broth

1 garlic clove, minced

¾ cup ketchup

1 tablespoon Dijon or yellow mustard

2 teaspoons brown sugar, granulated sugar, or honey

2 teaspoons Worcestershire sauce

¼ teaspoon fine sea salt

½ teaspoon hot sauce (optional)

4 soft hamburger buns

When I'm craving comfort food, sloppy Joes always hit the spot. If you're a fan, give this recipe a try—it comes together quickly and tastes way better than the canned stuff.

1. PREPARE THE FILLING. Select Sauté and adjust the heat to Medium. Put about ½ cup of the ground beef in the pot and let it cook, undisturbed, for about 4 minutes, or until very brown on the bottom. Add the onion and bell pepper and stir to scrape up the beef. Add the water and stir, scraping up any remaining browned bits from the pot. Add the remaining beef and cook, stirring to break up the meat, for about 3 minutes, until well browned. Add the garlic, ketchup, mustard, brown sugar, Worcestershire sauce, and salt. Stir to combine.

2. PRESSURE COOK. Lock the lid into place and turn the valve to "sealing." Select Pressure Cook and adjust the pressure to High. Set the time for 12 minutes. When cooking ends, carefully turn the valve to "venting" to quick release the pressure.

3. FINISH THE SLOPPY JOES. Unlock and remove the lid. Use a paper towel to blot the excess fat from the top of the meat mixture. Stir in the hot sauce (if using). If the sauce is very thin, select Sauté and adjust the temperature to Medium. Simmer the mixture until it reaches your preferred consistency. Spoon the meat and sauce onto the buns.

HAMBURGER STROGANOFF

Prep time: 10 MINUTES   *Sauté:* 7 MINUTES ON MEDIUM   *Pressure cook:* 8 MINUTES ON HIGH
Release: NATURAL FOR 5 MINUTES   *Total time:* 40 MINUTES

SERVES 6

EQUIPMENT
Measuring cups and spoons, chef's knife, can opener

Nonstick cooking spray

1 pound ground beef

1 small onion, minced

1 garlic cloves, minced

3 cups low-sodium beef broth

1 (10-ounce) can condensed cream of mushroom soup

1 teaspoon fine sea salt

¼ teaspoon ground black pepper

1 tablespoon all-purpose flour

3 cups dried egg noodles

1 cup sour cream

Stroganoff is my son Jacob's favorite. He requested that this book include this recipe. It's an easy dinner recipe with just one pot to clean. It's ground beef, seasoned just right, and egg noodles, all smothered in a rich brown gravy enriched with sour cream.

1. **SAUTÉ THE BEEF AND ONION.** Spray the inner cooking pot with nonstick cooking spray and select Sauté. Adjust the heat to Medium. Add the ground beef, onion, and garlic and cook for 7 minutes, or until the beef is browned and the onion is semi-translucent.

2. **ADD THE REMAINING INGREDIENTS.** Add the broth, stirring to loosen any ingredients that may have stuck to the bottom of the pot. Stir in the soup, salt, pepper, and flour and stir until smooth. Add the noodles.

3. **PRESSURE COOK.** Lock the lid into place and turn the valve to "sealing." Select Manual or Pressure Cook and adjust the pressure to High. Set the time for 8 minutes. When cooking ends, let the pressure release naturally for 5 minutes, then turn the valve to "venting" to quick release the remaining pressure.

4. **FINISH THE DISH.** Unlock and remove the lid and stir in the sour cream.

FRENCH DIP SANDWICHES

Prep time: 5 MINUTES   *Sauté:* 11 MINUTES ON HIGH   *Pressure cook:* 90 MINUTES ON MEAT
OR STEW   *Release:* NATURAL FOR 10 MINUTES   *Total time:* 2 HOURS 6 MINUTES

SERVES 6 TO 8

DAIRY-FREE OPTION

EQUIPMENT
Measuring cups and
spoons, chef's knife,
can opener

1 tablespoon olive oil

3 pounds beef chuck roast

2 teaspoons fine sea salt

1 teaspoon ground
black pepper

1 garlic clove, minced
(optional)

1 small onion, chopped

1 tablespoon
Worcestershire sauce

1 (10-ounce) can
condensed French
onion soup

1 (10-ounce) can
low-sodium beef broth

2 bay leaves (optional)

Sandwich rolls

Provolone cheese slices
(optional)

I am certain that this sandwich recipe has saved my college kids from starvation. It takes a while to cook, but once it's done, all you have to do is assemble the sandwich. It makes a lot, too, so you can use leftover meat in place of ground beef in Taco Pie (page 94), in place of the shredded chicken in Chicken Enchilada Soup (page 52), or to top a salad. You can also use the leftover juice in the bottom of the pot (called *jus*) in place of water for cooking rice or in place of the water and seasoning packet when cooking instant ramen.

1. BROWN THE BEEF. Select Sauté and adjust the heat to High. Add the oil to the inner cooking pot and allow it to heat for 1 minute. Season the roast with the salt and pepper. Add the meat to the pot and cook for about 5 minutes on each side to brown. Add the garlic (if using), onion, Worcestershire sauce, French onion soup, broth, and bay leaves (if using) to the pot.

2. PRESSURE COOK. Lock the lid into place and turn the valve to "sealing." Select Meat or Stew. Set the time for 90 minutes. When cooking ends, let the pressure release naturally for 10 minutes. If you are in class or away, it's okay to allow the pressure to release for longer.

3. FINISH THE MEAT. Unlock and remove the lid. Remove the roast and shred the meat using two forks or an electric hand mixer (see tip).

4. ASSEMBLE THE SANDWICHES. Slice the rolls in half lengthwise. Add the cheese (if using) and top with the shredded meat. Serve with the jus for dipping.

Cooking tip:

If you have a hand mixer, you can use it to easily shred the meat. Place the meat in a large bowl and set the beaters on the meat. Turn the beaters slowly to shred the meat.

TACO PIE

Prep time: 10 MINUTES   *Sauté:* 7 MINUTES ON MEDIUM   *Pressure cook:* 17 MINUTES ON HIGH
Release: NATURAL FOR 10 MINUTES   *Total time:* 54 MINUTES

SERVES 6

EQUIPMENT
Measuring cups and spoons, can opener, wooden spoon or silicone spatula, trivet, small bowl, mixing spoon, 7-inch springform pan, aluminum foil

1 pound ground beef

1 packet taco seasoning mix (see tip on page 90 for homemade)

1½ cups water

1½ cups canned refried beans (see tip on page 38 for homemade)

⅓ cup salsa

Nonstick cooking spray

4 (8-inch) flour tortillas

¼ cup enchilada sauce

2½ cups shredded sharp Cheddar cheese, divided

Optional taco toppings: shredded lettuce, chopped tomato, sliced avocado, etc.

Taco Tuesday has long been my family's favorite. I love it, too, but I realize that a small college kitchen can put a damper on the DIY taco bar setup. This one-pot recipe solves the small-space problem. Layers of tortillas, refried beans, salsa, seasoned ground beef, and cheese provide all of the taco bowl flavors and textures in a bowl.

1. BROWN THE BEEF. Select the Sauté setting and adjust the heat to Medium. Add the ground beef to the inner cooking pot and cook, stirring in the taco seasoning about halfway through the cooking time, until the meat is browned, about 7 minutes. Transfer the meat to a plate. Wash out the inner cooking pot and return it to the base. Put a trivet in the bottom, then pour in the water.

2. ASSEMBLE THE TACO PIE. In a small mixing bowl, combine the refried beans and salsa until well combined. Spray a 7-inch springform pan with nonstick cooking spray. Place one flour tortilla in the bottom of the pan. Spread ½ cup of the bean mixture on top of the tortilla, spreading it to the edges with a spatula or spoon. Add 1 cup of the ground beef, spreading evenly. Add the enchilada sauce and 1 cup of cheese. Place the second tortilla in the pan, topping and spreading with ½ cup refried beans, 1 cup meat, and then ½ cup cheese. Place the third tortilla in the pan, followed by ½ cup refried beans, 1 cup meat, then ½ cup cheese. Top with the last tortilla. Cover the pan with aluminum foil.

3. PRESSURE COOK. Use a sling (see page 17) to lower the taco pie onto the trivet. Lock the lid into place and turn the valve to "sealing." Select Manual or Pressure Cook and adjust the pressure to High. Set the time for 17 minutes. When cooking ends, let the pressure release naturally for 10 minutes.

4. GARNISH THE PIE. Using the sling, lift the pan out of the pot. Remove the foil. Remove the pie from the springform pan. Top with the remaining ½ cup of cheese and garnish with your favorite toppings.

Variation tip:

If you don't want to use beef, substitute ground turkey or chicken. This will make the dish a bit lighter.

MEATLOAF

10/19
Good

Prep time: 10 MINUTES   *Sauté:* 5 MINUTES ON MEDIUM   *Pressure cook:* 32 MINUTES ON HIGH
Release: QUICK   *Total time:* 57 MINUTES

SERVES 6

EQUIPMENT
Measuring cups and spoons, chef's knife, large bowl, medium bowl, mixing spoon, trivet, aluminum foil, instant-read meat thermometer

FOR THE VEGETABLES

2 tablespoons olive oil

10 small potatoes, quartered

1 (10 ounce) bag baby carrots

2 onions, quartered

Fine sea salt

Ground black pepper

1 cup low-sodium beef broth

This is the meal that started my love affair with the Instant Pot®. It's a one-pot meal with perfect potatoes (you can eat them as is or mash them for creamy mashed potatoes), carrots, and onions for the sides, and a moist, delicious meatloaf with a caramelized topping as the star attraction! The sauce is optional, but it adds a whole extra layer of flavor.

1. SAUTÉ THE VEGETABLES. Select Sauté and adjust the heat to Medium. Add the oil to the inner cooking pot. When the oil is hot, add the potatoes, carrots, and onions. Season with salt and pepper and sauté for 5 minutes. Add the broth. Turn the Instant Pot® off.

2. MAKE THE MEATLOAF. In a large mixing bowl, combine the beef, bread crumbs, cheese, eggs, onion, garlic, steak seasoning, salt, and pepper. Mix with your hands until well combined. Form the mixture into a round loaf shape. If you're planning to make the sauce, use your fingers to make an indentation on top of the meatloaf, leaving a ½ inch border around the meatloaf (it will look like a crater).

3. MAKE THE SAUCE (IF USING). In a medium bowl, stir together the ketchup, Worcestershire sauce, brown sugar, and mustard until the sugar dissolves. Pour this sauce into the crater you created on the meatloaf.

4. PRESSURE COOK. Spray a trivet on both sides with nonstick cooking spray and place it in the inner cooking pot, on top of the sautéed vegetables. Use a sling (see page 17) to place the meatloaf on top of the trivet. Lock the lid into place and turn the valve to "sealing." Select Manual or Pressure Cook and adjust the pressure to High. Set the time for 32 minutes. *35* When cooking ends, turn the valve to "venting" to quick release the pressure.

used my recipe — own recipe
Worcestershire Sauce

FOR THE MEATLOAF

2 pounds ground beef

1½ cups panko or
regular bread crumbs

None
1 cup grated
Parmesan cheese

Dried
~~2~~ 4 large eggs

1 small onion, minced

1 garlic clove, minced

1 teaspoon steak
seasoning (such as
McCormick's)

1 teaspoon fine sea salt

1 teaspoon ground
black pepper

Nonstick cooking spray

FOR THE SAUCE (OPTIONAL)

⅔ cup ketchup

2 teaspoons
Worcestershire sauce

5 teaspoons
brown sugar

1 tablespoon
ground mustard

5. FINISH THE MEATLOAF. Unlock and remove the lid. Use a meat thermometer to check the center of the meatloaf. It should register at least 160°F. Depending on the size and shape, you may need to seal the pot again and pressure cook for another 2 minutes or so. Once done, use the sling to remove the meatloaf from the pot. Let it rest for 5 minutes and then cut it into thick slices.

6. FINISH THE POTATOES. You have a difficult decision to make: Are you having mashed potatoes or roasted potatoes with your meatloaf tonight? See the tip below for how to make mashed potatoes. If you're having roasted potatoes, just spoon them on to your plate with the carrots and onions.

Variation tip:

To make mashed potatoes, remove the carrots and onions from the pot. Add 4 tablespoons unsalted butter to the pot with the potatoes and use a potato masher to mash the potatoes to the desired consistency. If they are too stiff, add a splash of milk and stir until you have the texture you like. You can season with additional salt and pepper.

Thanksgiving Turkey and Gravy (page 84), Cranberry Sauce (page 110), Mashed Potatoes (page 104), and Holiday Stuffing (page 109)

CHAPTER 8

Potlucks, Picnics, and Holidays

SPINACH-ARTICHOKE DIP

Prep time: 10 MINUTES   *Microwave:* 2 MINUTES   *Pressure cook:* 10 MINUTES ON HIGH
Release: QUICK   *Total time:* 32 MINUTES

SERVES 6

GLUTEN-FREE OPTION
VEGETARIAN OPTION

EQUIPMENT
Measuring cups and
spoons, pressure-safe
6-inch bowl, trivet, wooden
spoon or silicone spatula,
aluminum foil, cooling rack

Nonstick cooking spray

1 cup water, for steaming

1 (14-ounce) jar marinated
artichoke hearts, drained
and chopped

1 (10-ounce) package
frozen chopped spinach,
thawed and squeezed to
remove excess moisture

2 garlic cloves, minced

8 ounces cream cheese

¼ cup sour cream

½ cup shredded
Parmesan cheese

1 cup shredded
mozzarella cheese

1 teaspoon Worcestershire
sauce (see tip)

½ teaspoon cayenne
pepper (optional)

My mom is an amazing cook. I remember being at a restaurant
with her, and she was eating an appetizer and telling me all of
the ingredients that were in it from taste. Honestly, I thought
she was being eccentric. Then she sent me the recipe and
challenged me to make it. Turns out, my mom's taste buds
were spot on and she had duplicated the restaurant's appetizer. I won't say that I have those skills, but my daughter
does think this dip is one of the best. We like it with chips or
baguette slices.

1. **PREPARE THE POT.** Grease a 6-inch bowl with nonstick
cooking spray. Place the trivet in the inner cooking pot. Add
the water to the pot.

2. **COMBINE THE INGREDIENTS.** In the prepared bowl, combine
all of the ingredients and mix until well incorporated. Use a
spoon or spatula to spread the mixture evenly in the bowl.
Cover the bowl with aluminum foil to keep the water out of
the spinach–artichoke dip. Using a sling (see page 17), lower
the bowl with the spinach mixture onto of the trivet.

3. **PRESSURE COOK.** Lock the lid into place and turn the valve
to "sealing." Select Manual or Pressure Cook and adjust the
pressure to High. Set the time for 10 minutes. When cooking
ends, carefully turn the valve to "venting" to quick release
the pressure.

4. FINISH THE RECIPE. Unlock and remove the lid. Use the sling to lift the bowl out of the pot and place on a cooling rack. Remove the foil from the bowl. Stir the dip to combine all of the ingredients.

Ingredient tip:

Worcestershire sauce is made from anchovies. Most store-bought Worcestershire sauces are not gluten-free, but the one from Lea & Perrins is a gluten-free option. If you don't have Worcestershire sauce or prefer a vegetarian substitution, for every tablespoon of Worcestershire sauce called for in a recipe, mix together 2 teaspoons soy sauce, ¼ teaspoon lemon juice, ¼ teaspoon granulated sugar, and ¼ teaspoon hot pepper sauce.

CORN ON THE COB

Prep time: 5 MINUTES   *Pressure cook:* 3 MINUTES ON HIGH   *Release:* QUICK
Total time: 18 MINUTES

SERVES 4

**GLUTEN-FREE
VEGETARIAN**

EQUIPMENT
Measuring cups and
spoons, trivet

3 cups hot water,
for steaming

1 teaspoon fine sea salt,
plus more for seasoning

4 ears corn, shucked
and halved

2 tablespoons unsalted
butter, melted

Corn on the cob is a perfect snack while you study or a side
to your favorite entrée. Add butter and salt, or dress it up for
Mexican street corn (see tip). When choosing ears of corn,
look for green husks that are tightly wrapped around the cob.
Pull the husk back a bit and look for bright, plump kernels
arranged tightly in rows. The silk should be soft, moist, and a
pale golden color. The more silk inside the husk, the better
the corn on the cob. Finally, flip the corn upside down and
make sure the stalk is still green.

1. **PREPARE THE INGREDIENTS.** Place a trivet in the inner
cooking pot and add the water, salt, and corn.

2. **PRESSURE COOK.** Lock the lid into place and turn the valve
to "sealing." Select Manual or Pressure Cook and adjust the
pressure to High. Set the time for 3 minutes. When cooking
ends, carefully turn the valve to "venting" to quick release
the pressure.

3. **FINISH THE RECIPE.** Unlock and remove lid. Remove the
corn on the cob, drizzle with the butter, and season with salt
to taste.

Variation tip:

Slather your cooked corn with a quick Mexican sauce
to turn it into Mexican street corn: Stir together 1/3 cup
mayonnaise, 1/3 cup sour cream, 1/2 cup crumbled feta
cheese, 1 tablespoon dried cilantro, 1 teaspoon chili
powder, and 1 tablespoon freshly squeezed lime juice.
This sauce can also be used on potatoes or mixed into
rice, and it makes an excellent vegetable dip.

POTATO SALAD

Prep time: 5 MINUTES   *Pressure cook:* 4 MINUTES ON HIGH   *Release:* QUICK

Total time: 19 MINUTES

SERVES 12

DAIRY-FREE
GLUTEN-FREE
VEGETARIAN

EQUIPMENT
Measuring cups
and spoons, chef's
knife, 2 small bowls,
steamer basket, tongs
(optional), medium bowl,
mixing spoon

1 cup water, for steaming

3 pounds red potatoes,
washed and quartered

2 large eggs, uncracked

⅓ cup mayonnaise

3 tablespoons dill
pickle juice

1 tablespoon
prepared mustard

1 teaspoon fine sea salt

½ teaspoon ground
black pepper

1 celery stalk, diced

4 scallions (white and light
green parts only), chopped

Potato salad is a great side dish, and the Instant Pot® makes it almost effortless. This recipe is an adaption of an old family recipe, my Grandma Charlotte's. The pickle juice is her secret ingredient. (Shh! Don't tell anyone I told you!) You can use any type of mustard you like or have on hand—yellow mustard, spicy brown mustard, or Dijon all work well.

1. PREPARE AN ICE BATH FOR THE EGGS. Fill a small bowl with ice and cold water.

2. PRESSURE COOK THE POTATOES AND EGGS. Pour the water into the inner cooking pot and place a steamer basket inside. Put the quartered red potatoes in the steamer basket. Place the whole eggs on top of the potatoes. Lock the lid into place and turn the valve to "sealing." Select Pressure Cook or Manual and adjust the pressure to High. Set the time to 4 minutes. When cooking ends, carefully turn the valve to "venting" to quick release the pressure.

3. CHILL AND PREPARE THE EGGS. Unlock and remove the lid and immediately transfer the eggs to the ice bath (they'll be very hot, so use tongs or a spoon). The eggs should be covered by the cold water. When cool enough to handle, peel the eggs and transfer the yolks to another small bowl. Chop the egg whites and put them in a medium mixing bowl.

4. MAKE THE DRESSING. Mash the egg yolks with a fork. Add the mayonnaise, dill pickle juice, mustard, salt, and pepper and mix well.

5. MAKE THE POTATO SALAD. Add the potatoes to the bowl with the egg whites. Add the celery and scallions. Add the egg yolk mixture to the potato salad. Stir until the potatoes are well coated. Refrigerate until ready to serve.

MASHED POTATOES

Prep time: 10 MINUTES   *Pressure cook:* 8 MINUTES ON HIGH   *Release:* QUICK
Total time: 28 MINUTES

SERVES 6

**GLUTEN-FREE
VEGETARIAN OPTION**

EQUIPMENT
Measuring cups and
spoons, chef's knife,
colander, 2 large bowls,
potato masher or
electric mixer

3 pounds russet potatoes,
peeled and quartered

3 garlic cloves, peeled
and smashed

1 cup low-sodium chicken
broth or water

½ cup half-and-half
or whole milk

3 tablespoons
unsalted butter

1 teaspoon fine sea salt

Ground black pepper

When I was a kid, we visited family friends who lived on a potato farm. I remember walking up and down the field and watching our friends unearth potatoes. It was magical. When I was in college, I realized how magical potatoes really are. They are affordable, available everywhere, and so versatile. My college roommate once asked what my one "desert island food" would be. It was an easy answer: potatoes. From the simple spud I could eat baked potatoes, mashed potatoes, potatoes au gratin, French fries, Potato Salad (page 103), hash browns, and more! These days, I'd want to take my Instant Pot® with me, too, so that I could make this super easy and delicious mashed potato recipe.

1. PRESSURE COOK. Combine the potatoes, garlic, and broth in the inner cooking pot. Lock the lid into place and turn the valve to "sealing." Select Manual or Pressure cook and adjust the pressure to High. Set the time for 8 minutes. When cooking ends, carefully turn the valve to "venting" to quick release the pressure.

2. MASH THE POTATOES. Drain the potatoes in a colander set over a large bowl, reserving most of the cooking liquid in the bowl. Transfer the potatoes to another large bowl and add the half-and-half and butter to them. Use a potato masher (or electric mixer) to mash the potatoes, adding the reserved cooking water a little at a time, until they are the texture you like. Season with the salt and pepper.

Variation tip:

Garnish your mashed potatoes with bacon, chives, sour cream, or whatever toppings make your mashed potatoes special.

BLACK-EYED PEAS WITH HAM HOCKS

Prep time: 2 MINUTES   *Pressure cook:* 25 MINUTES ON HIGH   *Release:* NATURAL FOR
20 MINUTES   *Total time:* 57 MINUTES

SERVES 6

DAIRY-FREE
GLUTEN-FREE

EQUIPMENT
Measuring cups and
spoons, chef's knife

1 pound dried
black-eyed peas

1 tablespoon vegetable oil

8 cups low-sodium chicken
broth or water

2 ham hocks, trimmed of fat

1 onion, chopped

1 garlic clove, minced

1 celery stalk, finely
chopped (optional)

½ teaspoon fine sea salt
(optional)

½ teaspoon ground
black pepper

Black-eyed peas are a New Year's Day tradition, at least in the
South. It seems to have started during a cold December 1864,
when all that was left behind as General William T. Sherman
marched his Union Army to the sea was silos of black-eyed
peas. Eating black-eyed peas on January 1 is thought to bring
luck in the new year—for your best chances, it's recommended you consume 365 of them, one for each day of the
coming year.

1. PRESSURE COOK. Rinse the beans and discard any that float.
Combine all of the ingredients in the Instant Pot®. Lock the lid
into place and turn the valve to "sealing." Select Manual or
Pressure Cook and adjust the pressure to High. Set the time
for 25 minutes. When cooking ends, let the pressure release
naturally for 20 minutes, then turn the valve to "venting" to
quick release the remaining pressure.

2. FINISH THE DISH. Unlock and remove the lid. Use a fork to
mash some of the beans against the side of the pot to thicken
the broth.

CHEESE GRITS

Prep time: 7 MINUTES   *Pressure cook:* 15 MINUTES ON LOW   *Release:* NATURAL FOR 10 MINUTES
Total time: 42 MINUTES

SERVES 4

GLUTEN-FREE

EQUIPMENT
Measuring cups
and spoons

1 cup coarsely ground
cornmeal

3½ cups water

1 teaspoon fine sea salt

½ teaspoon ground
black pepper

4 tablespoons (½ stick)
unsalted butter

1 cup shredded sharp
Cheddar cheese

When I was 13, we moved to the South and I got an introduction to Southern hospitality and food. Grits quickly became a favorite. Recently, I taught my cousins, Louise and Shelley, how to eat grits. Some people like to add milk and sugar, but I prefer mine with cheese and butter.

1. PRESSURE COOK. Combine the cornmeal, water, salt, pepper, and butter in the inner cooking pot. Lock the lid into place and turn the valve to "sealing." Select Manual and adjust the pressure to Low. Set the time for 15 minutes. When cooking ends, let the pressure release naturally for 10 minutes, then turn the valve to "venting" to quick release the remaining pressure.

2. FINISH THE GRITS. Unlock and remove the lid and stir in the cheese.

Variation tip:

These grits also pair well with shrimp; however, you'll want to cook the shrimp separately and not in the Instant Pot® for best results.

BUFFALO CHICKEN WINGS

Prep time: 10 MINUTES   *Pressure cook:* 10 MINUTES ON HIGH   *Release:* QUICK
Total time: 30 MINUTES

SERVES 6

GLUTEN-FREE

EQUIPMENT
Measuring cups and spoons, chef's knife, trivet, large bowl, mixing spoon, tongs

1 cup water, for steaming

3 pounds chicken wing pieces, separated at joints

1 cup (2 sticks) unsalted butter, melted

1 cup hot sauce (such as Frank's RedHot)

2 tablespoons apple cider vinegar

Blue cheese dressing, for serving (optional)

You don't need to tailgate to whip up a batch of these mouthwatering chicken wings. The Instant Pot® turns out juicy, tender, delicious wings that fall off the bone. They're easy to make and feed the craving with the irresistible combination of vinegar and heat. Add a side of blue cheese dressing to cool the burn. The best part? These take only about 10 minutes in the Instant Pot®.

1. PRESSURE COOK. Place a trivet in the inner cooking pot and add the water. Pile the wings on top of the trivet. Lock the lid into place and turn the valve to "sealing." Select Manual or Pressure Cook and adjust the pressure to High. Set the time for 10 minutes. When cooking ends, carefully turn the valve to "venting" to quick release the pressure.

2. MAKE THE SAUCE. While the chicken is cooking, make the sauce by mixing the butter, hot sauce, and vinegar in a large bowl until well blended.

3. FINISH THE WINGS. When the wings are cooked, add them to the sauce and toss to coat. I find it is easiest to lift them out with tongs. Serve with blue cheese dressing (if using).

Variation tip:

If you have an oven, running the wings under a broiler after coating them with the sauce makes them extra tasty. Line a rimmed baking sheet with aluminum foil. Arrange the cooked and sauce-coated wings in a single layer on the baking sheet. Broil the wings for 5 minutes. Remove from the broiler and return them to the bowl of sauce. Place the wings back on the baking sheet in single layer. Broil for 5 more minutes. They should be lightly browned. I like to coat the wings one more time with the sauce before serving.

BBQ RIBS

Prep time: 25 MINUTES   *Broil:* 10 MINUTES   *Pressure cook:* 20 MINUTES ON HIGH
Release: NATURAL FOR 10 MINUTES   *Total time:* 1 HOUR 15 MINUTES

SERVES 4

DAIRY-FREE

EQUIPMENT
Measuring cups and spoons, chef's knife, trivet, tongs, rimmed baking sheet with rack

1 (3-pound) rack spareribs

½ teaspoon fine sea salt

1 cup water, for steaming

½ cup barbecue sauce

When you're in the mood for barbecued ribs but don't have all day to grill them—or don't have a grill—the Instant Pot® comes to the rescue! In a little over an hour, you can sit down to a platter of sticky, tender, delicious ribs. No grill required.

1. PREPARE THE RIBS. If desired, remove the membrane from the bone side of the rack of ribs, or cut through it every couple of inches. Sprinkle on both sides with the salt. Cut the rack into 3 pieces.

2. PRESSURE COOK. Pour the water into the inner cooking pot. Place a trivet in the pot and place the ribs on top of the trivet, stacking them if necessary. Lock the lid into place and turn the valve to "sealing." Select Manual and adjust the pressure to High. Set the time for 20 minutes. When cooking ends, let the pressure release naturally for 10 minutes, then turn the valve to "venting" to quick release the remaining pressure. Unlock and remove the lid. Use tongs to transfer the ribs, bone-side up, to a rack set over a rimmed baking sheet.

3. FINISH THE RIBS. Preheat the broiler and move the oven rack to the highest position. Baste the bone side of the rib sections with about half of the barbecue sauce and place under the broiler for 3 to 5 minutes, until browned and bubbling. Turn the ribs over and baste the other side with the remaining sauce. Return to the oven and broil for another 3 to 5 minutes.

Ingredient tip:

If possible, buy St. Louis—style spareribs. They're butchered to remove the irregular end of the rack that's striped with cartilage, so they're easier to cut up and easier to eat. Back ribs can be substituted with no change in the cooking time or method.

HOLIDAY STUFFING

Prep time: 7 MINUTES   *Sauté:* 3 MINUTES ON MEDIUM   *Pressure cook:* 15 MINUTES ON HIGH
Release: QUICK   *Total time:* 35 MINUTES

SERVES 6

VEGETARIAN OPTION

EQUIPMENT
Measuring cups and spoons, chef's knife, 6-inch cake pan, springform pan, or stainless steel bowl, wooden spoon or silicone spatula, large bowl, aluminum foil, trivet

Nonstick cooking spray

½ cup (1 stick) unsalted butter

1 small onion, chopped

2 celery stalks, chopped

1¼ cups low-sodium chicken or vegetable broth

1 (15-slice) loaf of bread, toasted if desired and cubed (about 9 cups)

2 teaspoons fine sea salt

¼ teaspoon ground black pepper

1 teaspoon dried sage

1 teaspoon dried oregano

1½ cups water, for steaming

Forget the boxed stuffing and make this easy, moist, and delicious homemade version part of your holiday traditions. Early in my relationship with my husband, I took pride in my stuffing—until one year when too many distractions had me adding way too much sage, making my stuffing inedible. It's the memory every holiday as I set the stuffing on the table and my husband asks for a "stuffing taster." This version has just the right amount of sage. You can use whatever bread you have on hand, or even mix the ends of several loaves.

1. PREPARE THE PAN. Grease a 6-inch cake pan, springform pan, or stainless steel bowl with nonstick cooking spray.

2. SAUTÉ THE VEGETABLES. Select Sauté and adjust the heat to Medium. Add the butter to the inner cooking pot. When it begins to foam, add the onion and celery. Stir for 3 minutes, until the onion is almost translucent. Stir in the broth.

3. MAKE THE STUFFING. In a large mixing bowl, toss the bread cubes with the salt, pepper, sage, and oregano. Pour the butter mixture over the bread and stir until the bread is coated. Transfer the stuffing to the prepared pan and use a spatula to spread it evenly. Cover the pan with aluminum foil. Poke a small hole in the center of the foil to allow it to vent. Wash out the inner cooking pot.

4. PRESSURE COOK. Pour the water into the inner cooking pot and place a trivet in the bottom. Using a sling (see page 17), lower the pan onto the trivet. Lock the lid into place and turn the valve to "sealing." Select Manual or Pressure Cook and adjust the pressure to High. Set the time for 15 minutes. When cooking ends, carefully turn the valve to "venting" to quick release the pressure.

5. FINISH THE RECIPE. Using the sling, lift the pan out of the pot. Remove the foil. Place a plate over the top of the pan and turn it upside down to release the stuffing onto the plate.

CRANBERRY SAUCE

Prep time: 5 MINUTES *Sauté:* 3 MINUTES ON NORMAL *Pressure cook:* 15 MINUTES ON HIGH
Release: NATURAL FOR 7 MINUTES *Total time:* 37 MINUTES

MAKES 2 CUPS

**DAIRY-FREE
GLUTEN-FREE
VEGETARIAN**

EQUIPMENT
Measuring cups
and spoons

¼ cup orange juice

1 teaspoon grated orange
zest (optional)

1 (12-ounce) bag whole
cranberries, rinsed and
sorted, divided

½ cup granulated sugar

When I was a child, we ate canned cranberry sauce and I never developed a taste for it. When I grew up, I simply left cranberry sauce off the holiday menu. Then I learned to make homemade cranberry sauce, which smells and tastes so much better than the canned stuff! Cranberry sauce brightens up a holiday plate, but it can also be used like jam on toast, to top a Cheesecake (page 114) or other dessert, or as an add-in for homemade Yogurt (page 24).

1. **GET READY TO COOK.** Combine the orange juice and orange zest (if using) and three-quarters of the cranberries in the inner cooking pot.

2. **PRESSURE COOK.** Lock the lid into place and turn the valve to "sealing." Select Manual or Pressure Cook and adjust the pressure to High. Set the time for 15 minutes. When cooking ends, let the pressure release naturally for 7 minutes, then turn the valve to "venting" to quick release the remaining pressure.

3. **FINISH THE RECIPE.** Unlock and remove the lid. Select Sauté and adjust the heat to Normal. Add remaining cranberries and the sugar. Stir until the sugar dissolves and the last berries begin to burst, about 3 minutes. Add a bit of water to thin the sauce out if it gets too thick for your liking.

Cooking tip:

Never do a quick release without first doing a natural release for at least 7 minutes. This sauce has a tendency to foam and spew.

GREEN BEAN CASSEROLE

Prep time: 15 MINUTES   *Sauté:* 4 MINUTES ON HIGH, 3 MINUTES ON MEDIUM
Pressure cook: 15 MINUTES ON HIGH   *Release:* QUICK   *Total time:* 47 MINUTES

SERVES 6

VEGETARIAN

EQUIPMENT
Measuring cups and spoons, wooden spoon or silicone spatula, small bowl

1 tablespoon olive oil

2 garlic cloves, minced

1 pound fresh green beans, trimmed

1 (10-ounce) can condensed cream of mushroom soup

½ teaspoon fine sea salt

¼ teaspoon ground black pepper

1 tablespoon all-purpose flour

¼ cup water

1 cup grated Parmesan cheese

½ cup shredded mozzarella cheese

⅓ cup plain bread crumbs

1½ cups crispy shoestring onions (optional)

This holiday, you and I will have something in common. We will each be remembering Dorcas Reilly. In a way, we invite her to our table whenever we serve green bean casserole: Dorcas Reilly is the home economist who created the infamous vegetable casserole that makes its appearance on tables across the country every holiday season. Reilly worked for the Campbell's Soup Company in the 1950s, creating and testing recipes in their New Jersey kitchen. Her inspiration for the dish was to create a quick and easy recipe around two things most Americans always had on hand in the 1950s: green beans and Campbell's Cream of Mushroom Soup.

1. **SAUTÉ THE GARLIC.** Select Sauté and set the heat to High. Add the oil to the inner cooking pot. After about 3 minutes, when the oil is hot, add the garlic and heat just until fragrant, about 1 minute.

2. **PRESSURE COOK.** Add the green beans and soup and stir to coat the green beans. Add the salt and pepper and stir to combine. Lock the lid into place and turn the valve to "sealing." Select Manual or Pressure Cook and adjust the pressure to High. Set the time for 15 minutes. When cooking ends, carefully turn the valve to "venting" to quick release the pressure.

3. **FINISH THE DISH.** Unlock and remove the lid. Select Sauté and adjust the heat to Medium. In a small bowl, mix the flour with the water to make a slurry. You want the slurry to be smooth and free of lumps. Pour the slurry into the pot and stir. Add the Parmesan cheese and stir for 2 minutes, until the cheese has melted. Add the mozzarella cheese to the top of the green beans. Don't stir; just let it melt on top. Sprinkle the bread crumbs and onions (if using) on top of the mozzarella cheese.

Cheesecake, mason jar variation (page 115)

Desserts

CHEESECAKE

Prep time: 10 MINUTES, PLUS 4 HOURS TO CHILL   *Pressure cook:* 35 MINUTES ON HIGH
Release: NATURAL FOR 20 MINUTES   *Total time:* 5 HOURS 5 MINUTES

SERVES 8

VEGETARIAN

EQUIPMENT
Measuring cups and spoons, 7-inch springform pan, parchment paper (optional), 2 large bowls, mixing spoon, electric mixer, silicone spatula, paper towels, aluminum foil, trivet

Nonstick cooking spray

1¼ cups crushed graham crackers (about 16 graham crackers)

4 tablespoons (½ stick) unsalted butter, melted

2 tablespoons granulated sugar

16 ounces cream cheese, at room temperature

½ cup brown sugar

¼ cup sour cream

1 tablespoon all-purpose flour

½ teaspoon fine sea salt

2 teaspoons vanilla extract

2 large eggs, at room temperature

2 cups water, for steaming

This cheesecake recipe has a creamy New York—style texture with a crumb crust and plenty of options. I'm providing a basic recipe, which you can consider a foundation for your imagination. When my daughter MacKenzie wanted to learn to cook, she chose cheesecake as her first recipe. Together we made this basic recipe and it was a hit! Then she started experimenting and creating new flavors (see the tips), and now she is a master of cheesecake. She says it is the dessert she will be known for. You can top this simple version with any toppings you like, such as such as fresh fruits, canned pie filling, caramel sauce, chocolate chips, or preserves.

1. **PREPARE THE PAN.** Grease a 7-inch springform pan with nonstick cooking spray. I recommend placing a piece of parchment paper on the bottom and greasing this as well.

2. **MAKE THE CRUST.** In a large mixing bowl, combine the graham cracker crumbs, butter, and granulated sugar and mix until moist. Pour the mixture into the prepared pan and press firmly to the bottom and up the sides about 2 inches.

3. **MAKE THE BATTER.** In another large mixing bowl, use an electric mixer to beat the cream cheese and brown sugar until creamy. Add the sour cream and mix, scraping the sides of the bowl. Add the flour, salt, and vanilla and stir to combine. Add the eggs, one at a time, and stir just until incorporated; do not overbeat. Pour the mixture into the prepared crust. Cover the pan with a paper towel and then aluminum foil.

4. **PRESSURE COOK.** Pour the water into the inner cooking pot and place a trivet in the bottom. Using a sling (see page 17), lower the pan onto the trivet. Lock the lid into place and turn the valve to "sealing." Select Manual or Pressure Cook and adjust the pressure to High. Set the time for 35 minutes. When cooking ends, let the pressure release naturally for 20 minutes, then turn the valve to "venting" to quick release the remaining pressure.

5. **CHILL THE CHEESECAKE.** Unlock and remove the lid. Using the sling, lift the pan out of the pot. Allow the cheesecake to cool on a cooling rack to room temperature and then refrigerated, still covered with foil, for at least 4 hours before serving.

Variation tips:

Make **mason jar cheesecakes** using six (½-pint) mason jars instead of a springform pan and omitting the crust. Add ½ cup batter to each jar and cover with foil. Arrange three jars on the trivet in the pot and stack the remaining three jars on top of them. Lock the lid into place, turn the valve to "sealing," select Manual or Pressure Cook, and adjust the pressure to High. Set the time for 8 minutes. When cooking ends, let the pressure release naturally for 15 minutes, then turn the valve to "venting" to quick release the remaining pressure. Let the jars cool on a rack and then refrigerate for at least 2 hours.

Make **chocolate cheesecake** by substituting chocolate wafer cookie crumbs for the graham cracker crumbs and adding 8 ounces melted chocolate chips to the batter. After the cheesecake has chilled, heat one (16-ounce) tub of chocolate frosting in the microwave for 5 seconds. Stir and pour over the top of the cheesecake.

Make **salted caramel cheesecake** by substituting crushed butter crackers for the graham cracker crumbs. Add 1 tablespoon caramel syrup to the batter, and top with dulce de leche and coarse sea salt.

PEACH AND BERRY COBBLER

Prep time: 5 MINUTES, PLUS 5 MINUTES TO REST   *Pressure cook:* 15 MINUTES ON HIGH
Release: NATURAL FOR 10 MINUTES   *Total time:* 45 MINUTES

SERVES 4

VEGETARIAN

EQUIPMENT
Measuring cups and spoons, 7-inch round cake pan, mixing spoon, medium bowl, small bowl whisk, aluminum foil, trivet

2 (21-ounce) cans peach pie filling

1 cup fresh berries

3 tablespoons unsalted butter, melted

1 large egg

½ cup Greek yogurt (see page 24 for homemade)

⅓ cup granulated sugar

½ teaspoon vanilla extract

1¼ cups all-purpose flour

2 teaspoons baking powder

1 cup water, for steaming

Cobbler provides all of the comfort and flavor of pie without the effort of making a crust. We love this cobbler recipe, which stars juicy peaches complemented by sweet berries. Try blueberries, blackberries, raspberries, or strawberries for a new flavor each time. Top with whipped cream or vanilla ice cream, if desired.

1. MIX THE FRUIT. Spread the peach pie filling in the bottom of a 7-inch round cake pan. Add the berries and gently fold them in.

2. MAKE THE TOPPING. In a medium bowl, stir together the butter, egg, yogurt, sugar, and vanilla. In a small bowl, whisk together the flour and baking powder, and add to the wet ingredients. Stir just until combined. The batter should be fairly stiff.

3. ASSEMBLE THE COBBLER. Spoon the topping over the top of the fruit. It's okay if the topping is slightly uneven or doesn't completely cover the fruit. Cover the pan with aluminum foil to prevent water from getting into the cobbler.

4. PRESSURE COOK. Place a trivet in bottom of the inner cooking pot and add the water. Using a sling (see page 17), lower the pan onto the trivet. Lock the lid into place and turn the valve to "sealing." Select Manual or Pressure Cook and adjust the pressure to High. Set the time for 15 minutes. When cooking ends, let the pressure release naturally for 10 minutes, then turn the valve to "venting" to quick release the remaining pressure.

5. FINISH THE RECIPE. Unlock and remove the lid. Using the sling, lift the cobbler out of the pot. Remove the foil and allow it to rest for 5 minutes.

Simplify it!

To make this even simpler, you can use a boxed cake mix for the topping. Just substitute one (15-ounce) box of white cake mix for the flour, sugar, baking powder, and salt. Mix the cake mix with the melted butter.

TURTLE BROWNIE PUDDING

Prep time: 5 MINUTES *Pressure cook:* 25 MINUTES ON HIGH *Release:* QUICK
Total time: 40 MINUTES

SERVES 4

VEGETARIAN

EQUIPMENT
Measuring cups and spoons, 7-inch round cake pan, medium microwavable bowl, mixing spoon, aluminum foil, trivet

Nonstick cooking spray

½ cup (1 stick) unsalted butter

8 ounces dark chocolate chips

1 cup granulated sugar

2 teaspoons vanilla extract

2 large eggs

¾ cup all-purpose flour

¾ cup pecans, chopped, divided

1 (12-ounce) jar caramel sauce, divided

1 cup hot water, for steaming

1 (12-ounce) jar hot fudge sauce

This dessert is everything I love: chocolate, caramel, pecans, and brownies. Irresistible, right? On lazy Sunday afternoons I often make my mom's brownie recipe. It takes me back to being a child, watching my mom bake brownies and play Scrabble with my dad at the kitchen table. We'd feast on the brownies warm out of the oven. This treat is just like that memory. Only in this recipe, the brownie is more like a gooey, sticky pudding.

1. PREPARE THE BATTER. Grease a 7-inch round cake pan with nonstick cooking spray. Combine the butter and chocolate chips in a medium bowl and melt them together in the microwave, stirring occasionally. Add the sugar and vanilla and stir until combined. Mix in the eggs, one at a time, stirring until no streaks of egg remain. Stir in the flour. Fold in ½ cup of pecans. Transfer the batter to the prepared pan. Add ¼ cup of caramel sauce and use a spoon to swirl it into the brownie batter. Cover the pan with aluminum foil.

2. PRESSURE COOK. Place a trivet in the inner cooking pot and add the water. Using a sling (see page 17), lower the pan onto the trivet. Lock the lid into place and turn the valve to "sealing." Select Manual or Pressure Cook and adjust the pressure to High. Set the time for 25 minutes. When cooking ends, carefully turn the valve to "venting" to quick release the pressure.

3. FINISH THE PUDDING. Unlock and remove the lid. Using the sling, remove the pan and then remove foil. The center will look undercooked, but it's okay. The consistency is going to be somewhere between a cake-like brownie and chocolate pudding. Allow it to cool. Drizzle with the remaining caramel sauce and the hot fudge and garnish with the remaining ¼ cup of pecans.

Ingredient tip:

Use ¾ cup homemade dulce de leche or a store-bought version in place of the caramel sauce.

Simplify it!

Use one (15-ounce) box of brownie mix in place of the sugar, chocolate chips, flour, and salt.

PUMPKIN PIE

Prep time: 10 MINUTES, PLUS 4 HOURS TO CHILL   *Pressure cook:* 35 MINUTES ON HIGH
Release: NATURAL FOR 10 MINUTES   *Total time:* 5 HOURS 5 MINUTES

SERVES 6

VEGETARIAN

EQUIPMENT
Measuring cups and spoons, can opener, small bowl, 7-inch springform pan, large bowl, whisk aluminum foil, trivet, cooling rack, plastic wrap

½ cup crushed graham crackers (about 7 graham crackers)

2 tablespoons unsalted butter, melted

½ cup brown sugar

1½ teaspoons pumpkin pie spice

½ teaspoon fine sea salt

1 large egg

1½ cups canned pumpkin purée

½ cup evaporated milk

1 cup water, for steaming

My grandmother makes an amazing pumpkin pie. I can remember boasting to my husband that her pumpkin pie was what every pumpkin pie dreamed it could be. The first Thanksgiving we spent with my grandmother, I kept telling him, "Wait until you taste Grandma's pumpkin pie!" When it was finally dessert time, my grandma cut him a big slab of pie and handed it to him. She was incredibly proud of the pie. He took a huge bite and looked at me. My grandma took a bite of the pie and exclaimed, "I left out the sugar!" That was the worst pumpkin pie, but through the years, Grandma's pie-making brought redemption. Top with dollops of whipped cream, if desired.

1. **MAKE THE CRUST.** In a small mixing bowl, combine the graham cracker crumbs and butter and mix until well combined. Press the mixture into the bottom and 1 inch up the sides of a 7-inch springform pan.

2. **MAKE THE FILLING.** In a large mixing bowl, combine the sugar, pumpkin pie spice, salt, egg, pumpkin purée, and milk. Whisk until well combined. Pour the filling into the prepared crust. Cover the pan with aluminum foil.

3. **PRESSURE COOK.** Place a trivet in the inner cooking pot and add the water. Using a sling (see page 17), lower the pan onto the trivet. Lock the lid into place and turn the valve to "sealing." Select Manual or Pressure Cook and adjust the pressure to High. Set the time for 35 minutes. When cooking ends, let the pressure release naturally for 10 minutes, then turn the valve to "venting" to quick release the remaining pressure.

4. **CHILL THE PIE.** Unlock and remove the lid. Using the sling, remove the pan from the pot and then remove the foil. Allow the pie to cool to room temperature on a cooling rack. Cover with plastic wrap and refrigerate for at least 4 hours before serving.

ARROZ CON LECHE

Prep time: 10 MINUTES   *Pressure cook:* 20 MINUTES ON PORRIDGE   *Release:* NATURAL FOR 10 MINUTES   *Total time:* 50 MINUTES

SERVES 6

<60 MINUTES
VEGETARIAN

EQUIPMENT
Measuring cups and spoons, can opener, mixing spoon

1 cup long-grain white rice, rinsed until the water runs clear

2 cups milk

1¼ cups water

2 tablespoons granulated sugar

⅛ teaspoon fine sea salt

1 (10-ounce) can sweetened condensed milk

1 teaspoon vanilla extract

One of my favorite meals quickly became arroz con leche (rice pudding). Creamy and sweet, it is the ultimate in comfort food. I got the recipe for it from my grandmother-in-law, but it was time-consuming and laborious to make. When I discovered that it is possible to make rice pudding in the Instant Pot®, I was beside myself and began making it regularly for my family. You can enjoy it warm or cold. When you store the rice pudding in the refrigerator, it will dry out a bit. Just add a little milk (or other liquid) and stir until it reaches your desired consistency.

1. **MIX THE INGREDIENTS.** Combine the rice, milk, water, sugar, and salt in the inner cooking pot and stir.

2. **PRESSURE COOK.** Lock the lid into place and turn the valve to "sealing." Select Porridge (this will set the time for 20 minutes). When cooking ends, let the pressure release naturally for 10 minutes, then turn the valve to "venting" to quick release the remaining pressure.

3. **FINISH THE RECIPE.** Stir in the sweetened condensed milk and vanilla. Serve warm or let cool to room temperature, cover, and refrigerate.

Variation tips:

Experiment with different flavors by adding raisins or other dried fruits, ground cinnamon or pumpkin pie spice, shredded coconut, orange zest, or jam, nuts, or maple syrup. Experiment with different types of milk (almond, coconut, etc.), too. Just don't use heavy cream, as it will curdle.

BREAD PUDDING

Prep time: 5 MINUTES   *Pressure cook:* 25 MINUTES ON HIGH   *Release:* NATURAL FOR 10 MINUTES   *Total time:* 50 MINUTES

SERVES 8

VEGETARIAN

EQUIPMENT
Measuring cups and spoons, bread knife, medium bowl, mixing spoon

2 cups milk

5 large eggs

⅓ cup granulated sugar

1 teaspoon vanilla extract

5 cups (about ½ loaf) cubed bread (2-inch cubes)

Nonstick cooking spray

2 tablespoons unsalted butter, cut into small pieces

Bread pudding is the best way I know to use up stale or leftover bread, but it works well with any bread you have. It's especially good with challah, brioche, or cinnamon raisin bread. You can find plenty of recipes for savory bread puddings, but in my house, we eat it strictly for dessert.

1. **MAKE THE PUDDING MIXTURE.** In a medium bowl, combine the milk, eggs, sugar, and vanilla and stir until the sugar dissolves. Add the bread cubes and stir to coat well. Refrigerate for 1 hour.

2. **PRESSURE COOK.** Grease the inner cooking pot with nonstick cooking spray. Pour in the bread mixture. Scatter the butter pieces on top. Lock the lid into place and turn the valve to "sealing." Select Manual or Pressure Cook and adjust the pressure to High. Set the timer for 25 minutes. When cooking ends, let the pressure release naturally for 10 minutes, then turn the valve to "venting" to quick release the remaining pressure.

3. **FINISH THE RECIPE.** Unlock and remove the lid. Allow the pudding to cool for a few minutes before serving.

> **Variation tip:**
>
> You can make a quick caramel sauce to top your bread pudding. Select Sauté on the Instant Pot® and add 4 tablespoons (½ stick) unsalted butter, ¼ cup brown sugar, and 1 teaspoon vanilla extract. Stir constantly until it thickens and begins to darken in color. Drizzle this syrup over the pudding.

APPLE DUMPLINGS

Prep time: 10 MINUTES   *Sauté:* 2 MINUTES ON MEDIUM   *Pressure cook:* 10 MINUTES ON HIGH
Release: NATURAL FOR 5 MINUTES   *Total time:* 37 MINUTES

SERVES 8

VEGETARIAN

EQUIPMENT
Measuring cups and spoons, chef's knife

1 (8-ounce) can refrigerated crescent rolls

1 large apple, peeled, cored, and cut into 8 wedges

4 tablespoons (½ stick) unsalted butter

½ cup brown sugar

2 teaspoons ground cinnamon

¼ teaspoon ground nutmeg

1 teaspoon vanilla extract

¾ cup orange juice

During my college years, I was a nanny. One summer, I traveled with the family to their home state of Pennsylvania and we drove through the Amish community just outside of Bethlehem. This recipe reminds me of that summer. Apple dumplings may have originated in Pennsylvania and are often consumed for breakfast; however, they make an exceptional dessert. I like them served warm and topped with ice cream. Sometimes I warm a can of cream cheese frosting in the microwave for 10 seconds, stir, and use a spoon to drizzle the frosting over the top of the dumplings before serving.

1. **PREPARE THE DUMPLINGS.** Open the can of crescent rolls and flatten the dough. Separate the 8 triangles. Place 1 apple wedge on each crescent roll triangle and fold the dough around the apple to enclose it.

2. **MAKE THE SAUCE.** Select Sauté and adjust the heat to Medium. Add the butter to the inner cooking pot. When it has melted, press Cancel and add the sugar, cinnamon, nutmeg, and vanilla, stirring until melted. Place the dumplings in the Instant Pot® (they should fit side by side) and drizzle with the orange juice.

3. **PRESSURE COOK.** Lock the lid into place and turn the valve to "sealing." Select Manual or Pressure Cook and adjust the pressure to High. Set the time for 10 minutes. When cooking ends, let the pressure release naturally for 5 minutes, then turn the valve to "venting" to quick release any remaining pressure. Unlock and remove the lid.

Ingredient tip:

Granny Smith, Gala, and Pink Lady apple varieties work well with this recipe.

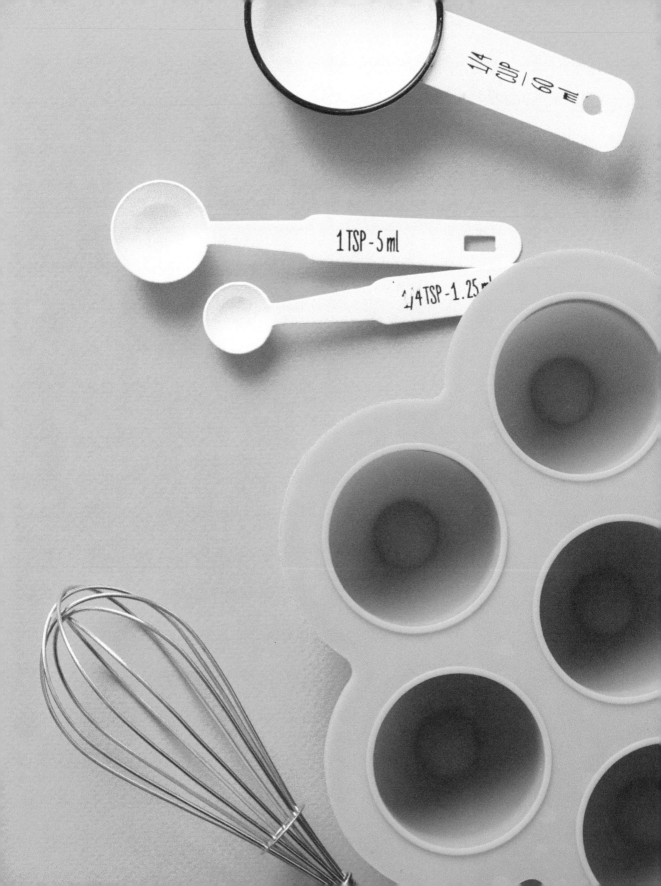

INSTANT POT® PRESSURE COOKING TIME CHARTS

The following charts provide approximate times for a variety of foods. To begin, you may want to cook for a minute or two less than the times listed; you can always simmer foods at natural pressure to finish cooking.

Keep in mind that these times are for the foods partially submerged in water (or broth) or steamed, and for the foods cooked alone. The cooking times for the same foods when they are part of a recipe may differ because of additional ingredients or cooking liquids, or a different release method than the one listed here.

For any foods labeled with "natural" release, allow at least 15 minutes natural pressure release before quick releasing any remaining pressure.

BEANS AND LEGUMES

When cooking beans, if you have 1 pound or more, it's best to use low pressure and increase the cooking time by a minute or two (with larger amounts, there's more chance for foaming at high pressure). If you have less than 1 pound, high pressure is fine. A little oil in the cooking liquid will reduce foaming. Unless a shorter release time is indicated, let the beans release naturally for at least 15 minutes, after which any remaining pressure can be quick released.

	MINUTES UNDER PRESSURE UNSOAKED	MINUTES UNDER PRESSURE SOAKED IN SALTED WATER	RELEASE	RELEASE
Black beans	22	10	High	Natural
	25	12	Low	
Black-eyed peas	12	5	High	Natural for 8 minutes, then quick
	15	7	Low	
Cannellini beans	25	8	High	Natural
	28	10	Low	
Chickpeas (garbanzo beans)	18	3	High	Natural for 3 minutes, then quick
	20	4	Low	
Kidney beans	25	8	High	Natural
	28	10	Low	
Lentils	10	not recommended	High	Quick
Lima beans	15	4	High	Natural for 5 minutes, then quick
	18	5	Low	
Navy beans	18	8	High	Natural
	20	10	Low	
Pinto beans	25	10	High	Natural
	28	12	Low	
Split peas (unsoaked)	5 (firm peas) to 8 (soft peas)	not recommended	High	Natural
Soybeans, fresh (edamame)	1	not recommended	High	Quick
Soybeans, dried	25	12	High	Natural
	28	14	Low	

GRAINS

To prevent foaming, it's best to rinse these grains thoroughly before cooking, or include a small amount of butter or oil with the cooking liquid. Unless a shorter release time is indicated, let the grains release naturally for at least 15 minutes, after which any remaining pressure can be quick released.

	LIQUID PER 1 CUP OF GRAIN	MINUTES UNDER PRESSURE	PRESSURE	RELEASE
Arborio (or other medium-grain) rice	1½ cups	6	High	Quick
Barley, pearled	2½ cups	10	High	Natural
Brown rice, medium grain	1½ cups	6—8	High	Natural
Brown rice, long grain	1½ cups	13	High	Natural for 10 minutes, then quick
Buckwheat	1¾ cups	2—4	High	Natural
Farro, whole grain	3 cups	22—24	High	Natural
Farro, pearled	2 cups	6—8	High	Natural
Oats, rolled	3 cups	3—4	High	Quick
Oats, steel cut	4 cups	12	High	Natural
Quinoa	2 cups	2	High	Quick
Wheat berries	2 cups	30	High	Natural for 10 minutes, then quick
White rice, long grain	1½ cups	3	High	Quick
Wild rice	2½ cups	18—20	High	Natural

MEAT

Except as noted, these times are for braised meats—that is, meats that are seared before pressure cooking and partially submerged in liquid. Unless a shorter release time is indicated, let the meat release naturally for at least 15 minutes, after which any remaining pressure can be quick released.

	MINUTES UNDER PRESSURE	PRESSURE	RELEASE
Beef, shoulder (chuck) roast (2 lb.)	35	High	Natural
Beef, shoulder (chuck), 2" chunks	20	High	Natural for 10 minutes
Beef, bone-in short ribs	40	High	Natural
Beef, flat iron steak, cut into ½" strips	1	Low	Quick
Beef, sirloin steak, cut into ½" strips	1	Low	Quick
Lamb, shoulder, 2" chunks	35	High	Natural
Lamb, shanks	40	High	Natural
Pork, shoulder roast (2 lb.)	25	High	Natural
Pork, shoulder, 2" chunks	20	High	Natural
Pork, tenderloin	4	Low	Quick
Pork, back ribs (steamed)	30	High	Quick
Pork, spare ribs (steamed)	20	High	Quick
Pork, smoked sausage, ½" slices	20	High	Quick

POULTRY

Except as noted, these times are for braised poultry—that is, partially submerged in liquid. Unless a shorter release time is indicated, let the poultry release naturally for at least 15 minutes, after which any remaining pressure can be quick released.

	MINUTES UNDER PRESSURE	PRESSURE	RELEASE
Chicken breast, bone-in (steamed)	8	Low	Natural for 5 minutes
Chicken breast, boneless (steamed)	5	Low	Natural for 8 minutes
Chicken thigh, bone-in	15	High	Natural for 10 minutes
Chicken thigh, boneless	8	High	Natural for 10 minutes
Chicken thigh, boneless, 1"–2" pieces	5	High	Quick
Chicken, whole (seared on all sides)	12–14	Low	Natural for 8 minutes
Duck quarters, bone-in	35	High	Quick
Turkey breast, tenderloin (12 oz.) (steamed)	5	Low	Natural for 8 minutes
Turkey thigh, bone-in	30	High	Natural

FISH AND SEAFOOD

All times are for steamed fish and shellfish.

	MINUTES UNDER PRESSURE	PRESSURE	RELEASE
Clams	2	High	Quick
Halibut, fresh (1" thick)	3	High	Quick
Large shrimp, frozen	1	Low	Quick
Mussels	1	High	Quick
Salmon, fresh (1" thick)	5	Low	Quick
Tilapia or cod, fresh	1	Low	Quick
Tilapia or cod, frozen	3	Low	Quick

VEGETABLES

The cooking method for all of the following vegetables is steaming; if the vegetables are cooked in liquid, the times may vary. Green vegetables will be tender-crisp; root vegetables will be soft. Unless a shorter release time is indicated, let the vegetables release naturally for at least 15 minutes, after which any remaining pressure can be quick released.

	PREP	MINUTES UNDER PRESSURE	PRESSURE	RELEASE
Acorn squash	Halved	9	High	Quick
Artichokes, large	Whole	15	High	Quick
Beets	Quartered if large; halved if small	9	High	Natural
Broccoli	Cut into florets	1	Low	Quick
Brussels sprouts	Halved	2	High	Quick
Butternut squash	Peeled, ½" chunks	8	High	Quick
Cabbage	Sliced	5	High	Quick
Carrots	½"–1" slices	2	High	Quick
Cauliflower	Whole	6	High	Quick
	Cut into florets	1	Low	Quick
Green beans	Cut in halves or thirds	1	Low	Quick
Potatoes, large russet (for mashing)	Quartered	8	High	Natural for 8 minutes
Potatoes, red	Whole if less than 1½" across, halved if larger	4	High	Quick
Spaghetti squash	Halved lengthwise	7	High	Quick
Sweet potatoes	Halved lengthwise	8	High	Natural

MEASUREMENT CONVERSIONS

Volume Equivalents (Liquid)

US STANDARD	US STANDARD (OUNCES)	METRIC (APPROXIMATE)
2 tablespoons	1 fl. oz.	30 mL
¼ cup	2 fl. oz.	60 mL
½ cup	4 fl. oz.	120 mL
1 cup	8 fl. oz.	240 mL
1½ cups	12 fl. oz.	355 mL
2 cups or 1 pint	16 fl. oz.	475 mL
4 cups or 1 quart	32 fl. oz.	1 L
1 gallon	128 fl. oz.	4 L

Oven Temperatures

FAHRENHEIT (F)	CELSIUS (C) (APPROXIMATE)
250°F	120°C
300°F	150°C
325°F	165°C
350°F	180°C
375°F	190°C
400°F	200°C
425°F	220°C
450°F	230°C

Volume Equivalents (Dry)

US STANDARD	METRIC (APPROXIMATE)
⅛ teaspoon	0.5 mL
¼ teaspoon	1 mL
½ teaspoon	2 mL
¾ teaspoon	4 mL
1 teaspoon	5 mL
1 tablespoon	15 mL
¼ cup	59 mL
⅓ cup	79 mL
½ cup	118 mL
⅔ cup	156 mL
¾ cup	177 mL
1 cup	235 mL
2 cups or 1 pint	475 mL
3 cups	700 mL
4 cups or 1 quart	1 L

Weight Equivalents

US STANDARD	METRIC (APPROXIMATE)
½ ounce	15 g
1 ounce	30 g
2 ounces	60 g
4 ounces	115 g
8 ounces	225 g
12 ounces	340 g
16 ounces or 1 pound	455 g

RECIPE INDEX

INDEX

ABOUT THE AUTHOR

Julee Morrison is a Virginia transplant who wants to taste the world and tell the stories of its food. Through her blog *Mommy's Memorandum*, she shares recipes for a wide range of Instant Pot® recipes as well as baked goods and desserts. She hopes someday to cook as well as her mom, make pie crust like Elsie the Great, pass on the stories told by her grandmother Charlotte the Great, and teach her children the secret ingredient in all dishes is love.

Julee is a mother of six: Jake (University of Utah), Kyra (Sacramento State University, magna cum laude), Zac, Abi, MacKenzie, and William. When she isn't cooking with her Instant Pot®, she travels, reads, blogs, paints, and cheers for her children.

Follow Julee online at MommysMemorandum.com and join her facebook community at facebook.com/MommysMemorandum.